TOMORROW IS SUNDAY

Sister Jean Daniel L.R.

Tomorrow is Sunday
The family prepares together for Mass

 St Paul Publications

ST PAUL PUBLICATIONS
SLOUGH   SL3 6BT   ENGLAND

Copyright © St Paul Publications 1977
Nihil obstat: D.A. Valente ssp
Imprimatur: F. Diamond vg, Northampton
First published November 1977
Printed in Great Britain by the Society of St Paul, Slough
ISBN 085439 141 X

CONTENTS

	Cycle A	Cycle B	Cycle C
18th Sunday of the Year	62	129	194
19th Sunday of the Year	63	130	196
20th Sunday of the Year	64	131	197
21st Sunday of the Year	66	133	198
22nd Sunday of the Year	67	134	200
23rd Sunday of the Year	68	135	201
24th Sunday of the Year	69	136	202
25th Sunday of the Year	71	138	204
26th Sunday of the Year	72	139	205
27th Sunday of the Year	73	140	206
28th Sunday of the Year	75	142	207
29th Sunday of the Year	76	143	209
30th Sunday of the Year	77	145	210
31st Sunday of the Year	78	146	212
32nd Sunday of the Year	80	147	213
33rd Sunday of the Year	81	148	214
Last Sunday of the Year	82	149	216

YEAR	CYCLE
1977	C
1978	A
1979	B
1980	C
1981	A
1982	B
1983	C
1984	A

εὐχαριστ
EUCHARIST
Thankyou

ACKNOWLEDGEMENTS

I should like to thank all those who have helped and encouraged me during the preparation of this book. Father Vincent Ryan worked with me in the initial stages when we were searching for ways to help parents with children in non-Catholic schools. He and Father Gabriel Leyden have made valuable suggestions.

Special thanks are due to Sisters Eileen Mary Cheek and Margaret Gardham for the illustrations and to Miss Irene Davies for all the typing involved.

Many other people have provided me with ideas, with the right word and with references. To these and to all the families and children who have given me inspiration, I am most grateful.

Introduction

WHY THIS BOOK?

The hour we spend at Mass on Sunday is the most important hour of the week. Here we are able to offer fitting worship and thanksgiving to God through the sacrifice of his Son, Our Lord Jesus Christ. Here we meet Our Lord and Saviour in a very special way in the Eucharist.

The Mass is prayer shared by each member of the family, no matter what his age. It is the great prayer of unity, to which we bring the love and service which is personal to us and which God expects from us.

SO

It seems right that we spend some time preparing for this great act of worship. The liturgy is one of the Church's ways of teaching us all. We want to prepare our hearts and minds to receive God's word so that we may respond to it. Week by week, we learn how to celebrate the death and resurrection of Jesus Christ with the Church, in our families and in our own lives.

WHO IS IT FOR?

It is for families — your family, my family. Older members will be able to contribute from their knowledge and experience and younger children will find a place in the activities.

WHAT YOU NEED

A Bible, Sunday Missal or a missalette collected in advance from your Parish Priest. The references are from the Jerusalem Bible. The places in the Bible should be marked with a book mark before the family meets together. The readings should be prepared so that they can be read with dignity and understanding.

HOW TO WORK

Every family is different, so the time and way of meeting will vary accordingly. Some time on Saturday seems the best. Occasionally the discussion can begin during a meal. One of the parents or an older child should guide the session and be responsible for preparing it in advance.

WHAT ARE WE AIMING AT?

We are hoping to draw the family together in prayer. We hope that each member will help the others to appreciate the Mass more and to become more ready to receive God's Word and Sacrament with faith and love. The exchange of experience and the sharing of thoughts on attitudes is an important part of our family preparation for Mass. We want to make the Mass a joyful celebration of our thankfulness to God for all his goodness to us.

Cycle A

JESUS BRINGS PEACE

Things you need

Your Advent wreath and matches.
Two book markers.

Prepare your Bible

Old Testament: Isaiah, ch. 2, vv. 1-5.
New Testament: St Matthew, ch. 24,
              vv. 37-44.

First Reading

Read the passage from Isaiah and see how full of hope it is for all men
— hope that God will live with his people, and hope that he will show
them how to live at peace with one another.

It is a vision of human life being made really human. Instruments of
death become tools to support life. Sin gives way to growth. Hatred
is absorbed and crushed by love. Human life is seen to become whole-
some in a community of mutual sharing and respect. The common life
of the community comes to flower and enriches the face of the earth.

This is PEACE. How can we work for peace this Advent — at home,
in school, at work?

Prayer

The reading ends with these words:
                 "O House of Jacob come,
                 Let us walk in the light of the Lord".

As you light the first candle of your Advent wreath and watch it burn,
use these two lines as a prayer — but change the name "Jacob" to your
own family name.

Gospel Reading

The special Advent phrase is "Stay awake". As you read the passage
from St Matthew, notice the people Jesus mentions who were caught off
their guard. How many can you find?

Jesus comes to us these days in many different ways and through many different people. How can we "stay awake" and recognise him when he comes?

To make an Advent wreath

You need a base of rolled newspaper or a wire coathanger bent into a circle. Cover your circle by binding on evergreen leaves — holly, ivy, laurel, yew, etc. Fix four candles firmly in the wreath. Sometimes a ribbon tied in a bow is used to decorate the wreath. (Blue Peter often explains a good way to make an Advent wreath.)

2nd Sunday of Advent   *Cycle A*

PREPARE THE WAY

Things you need

Advent wreath and matches.
Pencil and paper.

Prepare your Bible

Old Testament:
        Isaiah, ch. 11, vv. 1-10.
New Testament:
        St Matthew, ch. 3, vv. 1-12.

First Reading

We can see how Isaiah expected God to bring his people peace and justice.

— Who was the famous son of Jesse? (See 1 Samuel, ch. 16, vv. 4-13.)
— What connection had he with Jesus? (Think of a well-known Christmas carol.)
— What gifts of the Holy Spirit are mentioned here?
— Write down the names of the 12 animals in this reading.
— How do these verses show the peace that comes when we let God rule our lives and hearts?

Gospel Reading

In this passage from St Matthew, one of the animals on your list is mentioned. Which is it?

— John was trying to help people to let God live in their hearts and to be present in their world. He told them that to be God's friends, it was not enough simply to claim that they were related to men like Abraham. God cannot give peace to those who love wrong-doing, even though they may be people who have a great knowledge of God and have very famous and holy ancestors. To let God ENTER is to let love enter. People must be prepared to let him influence their attitudes and choice, their thoughts and actions. The SIGN of being prepared to change and to let God "take over" was to allow John the Baptist to bury one in the waters of the River Jordan. It was a kind of action-prayer, asking God to let the devil in one's heart die and to give place to a new way of living. Jesus, when he preached, made the same call to men.

— We are getting ready for Christmas. We want to prepare the way for Jesus Christ to come more fully into our lives and hearts.

— Light two candles of your Advent wreath. Let us think how we can prepare our hearts to give him a loving welcome:

> — by trying to be more forgiving,
> — by trying to think of others before ourselves,
> — by taking more care when we pray,
> — . . . .

3rd Sunday of Advent   *Cycle A*

BE GLAD

Things you need
Your Advent wreath and matches.

Prepare your Bible
Old Testament:
    Isaiah, ch. 35, vv. 1-6, 10.

First Reading
(For young members of the family
— Have you planted any bulbs this
year? Can you think of a place in your garden or in the park where you *know* there will be daffodils in the spring?)

15

(For older members — Can you think of expressions where we use words like "blossoming", "budding", to describe growth in friendship or joy?)

— As you read the passage from the prophet Isaiah, notice how many words there are about happiness.
— have your hands ever been tired?
— Have your knees ever trembled?
— Have you ever shouted for joy? Share your experiences.

Lighting the Candles

When we light the three candles on our wreath, perhaps we could thank God quietly for the eyes to see them, for the steady hand to hold the match, for our ears to hear the sounds around us.

Could our family do anything this Christmas to help a handicapped person?

Prayer

Here is a prayer written in the 16th century by St Teresa of Avila. We could say it slowly, perhaps more than once.

> Christ has
> no body on earth but yours;
> no hands but yours
> no feet but yours.
> Yours are the eyes
> through which is to look out
> Christ's compassion to the world.
> Yours are the feet
> with which he is to go about
> doing good.
> Yours are the hands
> with which he is to bless men now.

MARY'S CHILD

Things you need

Your Advent wreath and matches. Write EMMANUEL in colour on a small card. Prepare to lead the "prayer" suggested below.

Prepare your Bible

New Testament: St Matthew, ch. 1, vv. 18-25.

Gospel Reading

Read the passage together and then concentrate on verse 23.

— We shall hear this name "Emmanuel" three times at Mass on Sunday. (If you have a young member in your family, he may like to take the card you have prepared and listen for the word each time it is spoken.)

— If you sing one particular Advent hymn, you will sing "Emmanuel" in the chorus after each verse. Which hymn is it?

Prayer

Turn off the lights in your room before lighting the four candles on your wreath. Wait quietly until your eyes are used to the candlelight.

Look at the candles or close your eyes. Think of the fact that you are in God's presence. You do not see him, but he is with you, keeping you alive and giving you all the gifts which are yours. If your mind begins to wander, simply say quietly, "Emmanuel. God is with us".

God is with us in our family because we love one another and God is love.

God is with each one of us because we are baptised and he lives in us.

God lived very specially in Mary while she was carrying Jesus and waiting for him to be born.

Say together the "Hail Mary" quite slowly. Notice the words the angel used to tell Mary that God was with her.

B

THE HOLY FAMILY

Things you need

Your favourite Christmas card showing the Holy Family. A photo of your own family.

Prepare your Bible

Old Testament: Ecclesiasticus, ch. 3, vv. 2-6, 12-14.
New Testament: Colossians, ch. 3, vv. 12-21.

First Reading

Read the passage together. Most of the reading concerns grown-up children and how they should take care of their parents as they grow old. Here are some thoughts for us all:

How do we show respect for each other in our home?
— in the way we talk to each other,
— in the way we treat each other's possessions,
— in the way we try to be sensitive to each other's needs.

How can we "put our mother at ease" when she is tired, or when she is worried, or when she is busy?

Second Reading

Look at the picture and the photo you have chosen while you listen to St Paul telling the people of Colossae what a family should be like.

Prayer

Either hold hands with each other or put your hands together and close your eyes. In turn pray for each member of the family, perhaps like this:

Dad: Thank you God, for Mummy, John, Susan and Peter.

Susan: God our Father, thank you for Mum and Dad, for John and Peter. Please bless us all.

And so on.

Finish by saying together the prayer Jesus taught us: Our Father . . .

GOD — REALLY WITH US

This is the first Sunday in the New Year and it may be the first time you have been to Mass in this New Year. The readings are full of wonder — difficult perhaps to understand, but they lead us to adore God who has come to dwell among us.

Prepare your Bible

Old Testament: Ecclesiasticus (or Sirach), ch. 24, vv. 1-4, 12-16.

Your Experience

Have you ever slept in a tent? Do you remember any of the places where you have camped and pitched your tent? Did it seem like a little home when you crept in at night or when it was raining?

First Reading

Read the passage together and find out:

vv. 4, 13 — Where was the tent pitched?

v. 12 — Who chose the place for the tent to be pitched?

What is the picture, drawn in words, trying to help us to understand?

God is expressing his mind / his thought / his Word } his wisdom } in Jesus

Jesus is the revelation of the Father. St John says: "No one has ever seen God; It is the only Son, who is nearest to the Father's heart, who has made him known".

Another Word

In v. 10, there is another word for tent — TABERNACLE. In Old Testament times, the tabernacle was the very special tent where the Law of God was kept. For the Jews, the Law of God was like a contract. It contained God's agreement to love them and his promise always to look after them like a father. The books kept in the tabernacle were the visible reminder of God's promise. They were a sign of his presence and his love.

— In our Catholic churches, what is the tabernacle? Who has the key?

19

Why must it be kept safe? Sometimes the tabernacle looks like a tent because it has a veil over it. How do we know that the Blessed Sacrament is in the tabernacle? Is the veil over the tabernacle always the same colour?

To think about

The tabernacle is the sign of God's presence with us, that his tent is still pitched among us, that he still cares for us, that he is still present.

Sunday after the Epiphany   *Cycle A, B, C*

JESUS IS BAPTISED
BY JOHN THE BAPTIST

Things you need

Anything you have to remind you of your baptism — certificate, photo, presents you received, anything you wore, small jug of water . . .

Preface of the Mass

Today we have a special Preface to introduce the heart of the Mass, the Eucharistic Prayer.

> Father, all-powerful and ever-living God,
> we do well everywhere and always to give you thanks.
>
> You celebrated your new gift of baptism
> by signs and wonders at the Jordan.
> Your voice was heard from heaven
> to awaken faith in the presence among us
> of the Word made man.
>
> Your Spirit was seen as a dove,
> revealing Jesus as your servant,
> and anointing him with joy as the Christ,
> sent to bring to the poor
> the good news of salvation.
>
> In our unending joy we echo on earth
> the song of the angels in heaven
> as they praise your glory for ever: Holy, holy, holy . . . .

Discuss

The day of the baptism of Jesus was a wonderful day for John the Baptist. What did John now know for sure about his cousin?

It was a great day for Jesus. He was to begin the work his Father had sent him to do. What does the Preface tell us that this work was?

Our baptism was a great day for us. Look at the reminders you have found. Ask your parents about your baptism day. Remember who your godparents were.

At our baptism we became members of a family who come together regularly to praise God. Each member of the family is anointed and chosen by God to be a person who will work like Jesus to bring happiness to our world by helping men to know God and to live in his way.

Prayer

Say together the Opening Prayer of the Mass:

> Almighty, eternal God,
> keep us, your children, born of water and the Spirit,
> faithful to our calling.
> Through Christ Our Lord.

1st Sunday of Lent   *Cycle A*

GOD IS EVERYTHING TO US

Preparation

Look around your house and find out what things you have in it, that were not to be found in your parents' homes when they were your age. Try to ask your grandparents the same question. What difference did it make to their lives? Can you imagine what it was like not to have biros, crisps, TV? Yet life was fundamentally the same — they were happy and sad, they ate and slept, they worked and played, they wrote letters and had family parties. They got married, had children and died.

Prepare your Bible

Old Testament: Genesis, ch. 2, vv. 7-9; ch. 3, vv. 1-7.
New Testament: St Matthew, ch. 4, vv. 1-11.

First Reading

This was written about 950 BC. It's difficult to imagine what life was like then — more difficult than imagining what life was like when your grandparents were young. But people must have asked the same kind of questions as we do.

What is the meaning of life?
What is the world like?
How should we live in it?

They came to three conclusions: God is with us. We must live as God's people. We spoil our happiness and that of others by choosing to live in a way forbidden by God. What do you think about that? Is it true for us today?

The story we read is an attempt to explain what the people were trying to understand. Underneath the story there is real and deep meaning — how easy it is for us to be tempted to do what gives us pleasure at the time!

Gospel Reading

Here is another story of someone who was tempted to make life easy for himself. Read it for yourselves. God had sent his Son into the world on a very special mission and Jesus wanted, above all else, to do what his Father trusted him to do.

In our lives

During the forty days of Lent, we try to become more like Jesus. This may mean doing some hard things in a loving way. We must not accept flattery if it takes us away from the truth that we belong to God.

Learn by heart

God made me to know him,
to love him and to serve him
in this world,
and to be happy with him
for ever in the next.

THE GLORY OF CHRIST

Things you need

A table lamp or torch or other light that you can direct on to the page of the Bible.

Prepare your Bible

Old Testament: Genesis, ch. 12, vv. 1-4.
New Testament: St Matthew, ch. 17, vv. 1-9.

First Reading

Abram lived in Ur when he began to hear God's call. Find out from the reading what God was asking him to give up.

— Did Abram know where he was going?

— How did Abram show faith in a God he had not seen?

His faith was rewarded many, many generations later. Abram was the first friend of God among the special people, the Jewish people, from whom Mary was to come to be the mother of his Son.

Let us pray for the grace to respond to the Word of God.

God our Father,
help us to hear your Son.
Enlighten us with your word,
that we may find the way to your glory. Amen.

Gospel Reading

Arrange your light so that it shines directly on the passage of St Matthew. Let someone take the part of Jesus and another member of the family read the part of Peter.

Discussion

— Which disciples were with Jesus to witness his glory?

— Which Old Testament people did they see?

— Peter, the impulsive one, suggests making tents. If you make a tent, what do you usually intend to do with it?

— At what other moment in the life of Jesus, did the voice of God say nearly the same words?
— Why were the disciples afraid?
— What gave them back their courage?
— Then they moved off with Jesus — it was not the moment to rest in tents. How does this link up with Abram?
— What did Jesus say to them as they came down the mountain that they would not have understood then, but only later?

LIVING WATER

Things you need

A jug of water and a glass; a clean handkerchief and a dirty one; a dry leaf and a fresh leaf. Pencil and paper.

Prepare your Bible

Old Testament: Exodus, ch. 17, vv. 3-7.
New Testament: St John, ch. 4, vv. 5-42.

(It would be a good idea for one member of the family to read this passage before you all meet, especially if there are young children.)

Introduction

In the early Church when most people became Christians when they were adults, there was only one moment in the year when they could be baptised. This was Easter night during the Vigil.

Lent was the very special final preparation for the catechumens (the name given to those preparing for Baptism). There were several steps to be taken by these "Christians-on-the-way" during Lent. The Mass on this Sunday concentrates on water and the use of it in baptism.

Entrance antiphon

(This is the verse we say or sing as the priest comes in to Mass.)

24

I will prove my holiness through you. I will gather you from the ends of the earth; I will pour clean water on you and wash away all your sins. I will give you a new spirit within you, says the Lord.

(As you read this antiphon, ask someone to pour water into the glass, to put the clean hanky in place of the dirty one, to put the fresh, living leaf in place of the dry, dead one.)

First Reading

When you read this, say why Moses felt he was in danger of being stoned. How did God come to his rescue?

New Testament

Ask one of the children to draw a well, then tell the story without the teaching of Jesus.

The disciples were surprised to find Jesus talking to the Samaritan woman:

a) because she was a woman,
b) because she came from Samaria, a country which strict Jews despised.

Discussion

Does this tell us anything about who should be baptised? How does it link up with the entry antiphon?

To think about

Here is just one thing Jesus said to the woman. "The water that I shall give will turn into a spring inside him, welling up to eternal life". Water used at baptism is a visible sign of something that we can't see but which is real. What is it?

25

LAETARE!

Things you need

A bottle of olive oil from the larder or medicine cupboard (if possible); sheep from your farmyard set, if you have one; some mud from the garden in a saucer. The Latin word LAETARE written on a piece of paper. Arrange all these things on the table.

Prepare your Bible

Old Testament: 1 Samuel, ch. 16, vv. 1, 6-7, 10-13.
New Testament: St John, ch. 9, vv. 1-41.
(This needs to be read by one of the family who can then tell the story.)

Opening prayer of the Mass

> Father of peace,
> we are joyful in your Word,
> your Son Jesus Christ,
> who reconciles us to you.
> Let us hasten towards Easter
> with the eagerness of faith and love.

Your Laudate card

This is the middle Sunday of Lent and we rejoice that we are halfway to Easter. How are the Lent resolutions going? When Mass was in Latin, this was called Laetare Sunday — we are encouraged to rejoice and to set aside our acts of penance today.

First Reading

Choose a narrator, the Lord, Samuel and Jesse to read the different parts. Ask your youngest member (if he is still quite young!) to have the sheep in front of him during the story.

Discussion

— Why were you asked to find some olive oil?
— What kind of horn was Samuel carrying?
— What does "anointing with oil" signify?

26

— We are told that "the Spirit of the Lord seized on David and stayed with him from that day on". What was the day when the Holy Spirit "seized" on us?

Gospel Reading

Tell the story if you have young children in your family.
— Why were you asked to bring some mud?
— Washing with water gave the man his sight — why do you think this reading was chosen specially for the catechumens?

Prayer after Communion

> Father,
> you enlighten all who come into the world.
> Fill our hearts with the light of your Gospel,
> that our thoughts may please you
> and our love be sincere.

5th Sunday of Lent   *Cycle A*

JESUS BRINGS LIFE

Things you need

A crucifix and a lighted candle together on a small cloth or mat or handkerchief.

Write carefully on a card:

> Jesus said: "I am the resurrection and the life;
> whoever believes in me will never die".

Prepare your Bible

New Testament: Romans, ch. 8, vv. 8-11;
             St John, ch. 11, vv. 1-45.
— When did the Spirit of God make his home in us?
— What outward sign do Catholics very often make, to show that they belong to Jesus Christ?

This sign is first made on the forehead of the Christian by the priest and then by the parents and godparents just before entering the church for baptism.

— What do Christians often wear to show that they belong to Christ? If any of you wear this sign, remember now who gave it to you and on what occasion.

— What sign is often put over the grave of a Christian to show they belong to Christ?

Gospel Reading

The incident that we read about in the Gospel today sparked off the final determination of the enemies of Christ to capture him, to find a way to do away with him. It concerns the death of Lazarus and the grief of his two sisters. This family were great friends of Jesus and he must often have stayed with them.

Sunday Preface

There is a special preface to introduce the Eucharistic Prayer this Sunday. Read it and think about it, and then join in the Holy, holy, holy,

Father, all-powerful and ever-living God,
we do well always and everywhere to give you thanks
through Jesus Christ Our Lord.

As a man like us, Jesus wept for Lazarus his friend.
As the eternal God, he raised Lazarus from the dead.
In his love for us all,
Christ gives us the sacraments
to lift us up to everlasting life.

Through him the angels of heaven offer their prayer of adoration
as they rejoice in your presence for ever.
May our voices be one with theirs
in their triumphant hymn of praise: HOLY, HOLY, HOLY . . . .

HOSANNA!

Things you need

A red cloth or mat or handkerchief or piece of paper. A small branch with green leaves (box is the traditional tree) for each member of the family. Make some tiny crowns with gold or silver paper or milk bottle tops to hang with cotton on your branches. A donkey from your farm-yard set if you have one.

Arrange all these things on the table where you are going to study together.

Prepare your Bible

Old Testament: Isaiah, ch. 50, vv. 4-7.
New Testament: St Matthew, ch. 21, vv. 1-11.

Prayer

(Hold your branch)

> Lord,
> increase the faith of your people
> and listen to our prayers.
> Today we honour Christ our triumphant King
> by carrying these branches.
> May we honour you every day
> by living always for him
> for he is Lord for ever and ever.

Gospel Reading

This passage from St Matthew will be read by the priest after he has blessed the palm branches and your own branches if you take them to Mass tomorrow.

— Read the passage together. Discover the different titles Jesus is
   given: M - - - - -   K - - -
              S - - of D - - - -
              P - - - - - -

— How did the crowds show that they believed Jesus was someone important?

— At what part of the Mass do we say "Hosanna?"

Say the "Holy, holy, holy" all together and compare it with what the people shouted as Jesus entered Jerusalem.

First Reading

What a contrast to what we have just read! Discuss how the things prophesied by Isaiah really happened to Jesus.

Things to do

If you have your palms left from last year, you should burn them today. They have been blessed so should not be thrown away. Take your decorated branches to Mass so that they can be blessed.

The blessed branch or palm should be put in a special place — behind your crucifix for example.

Easter Sunday   **Cycle A, B, C**

ALLELUIA!

Things you need

A candle (new if possible) in a dish (coleslaw or margarine container is suitable) that can hold water. A small clean empty bottle with a screw top: stick a white cross of paper on it if you haven't a Holy Water bottle already. Make a small cross from two twigs tied together for each member of the family.

Prepare your Bible

New Testament: St John, ch. 20, vv. 1-9.

Celebration

      Leader—We are meeting today for a very special preparation for our Sunday Mass. Some of us (name them) will be going to the Easter Vigil this evening so that we can watch and pray and wait for the first moments of Easter Day when we welcome our Risen Lord.

    1st child—Today, Holy Saturday, we think of the empty crosses (all hold the crosses you have made) on the hill of

Golgotha. We think of the sadness of Our Lady and the despair of Peter and the apostles.

2nd child—We are Christians who know what was going to happen very early in the morning. Here is our candle waiting to be lit to show the new and everlasting life of Jesus Christ. Tomorrow we will light it and we will put flowers round it to show our joy in the new life Jesus brought for us.

3rd child—Here is our bottle in which we shall collect the Easter water which will be blessed during the Vigil. The water reminds us of our baptism and the new life which was given to us then.

Leader—Let us read the account St John gives us of those early moments on the first Easter Day.

Gospel Reading
All stand.

Prayer

God our Father,
by raising Christ your Son you conquered the power of death
and opened for us the way to eternal life.
Let our celebration tomorrow raise us up and renew our lives
by the Spirit that is within us. AMEN.

Things to do

Try to leave your Bible open with the things you have used for the celebration beside it. Pick some little flowers ready to put in water round your candle tomorrow. Remember to take your bottle to church to collect your Easter water.

PEACE BE WITH YOU

Things you need
Your Easter candle with flowers on a white mat or cloth. Matches. Any Easter cards you have received. Some holy water in a small glass dish or a Holy Water stoup if you have one.

Prepare your Bible
New Testament: Acts, ch.2, vv. 42-47;
St John, ch. 20, vv. 19-31.

To begin
Light your candle and sign yourselves with Holy Water.

First Reading
The first Christians were Jews who had responded to the teaching of the apostles and had asked for baptism. Read the passage together.
What city were these converts living in? (Clue — the mention of the Temple.)
How are we faithful to these same four things in our parish:—
    a) The teaching of the apostles
    b) The brotherhood
    c) The breaking of bread
    d) The prayers?
How did the first Christians show they cared for each other?

Gospel Reading
Before you read the Gospel turn the key in your door or bar it in some way.
What was the greeting of Jesus to the disciples on both occasions?
What priestly power did the Risen Lord give the disciples on Easter evening?
What did Thomas say when he was convinced that Jesus was truly alive?
Some people like to say in their hearts this same phrase at Mass. It expresses their faith in the Risen Lord present with us.

Blessing

(said by Father or Mother)
> Through the resurrection of his Son
> God has redeemed us and made us his children.
> May he bless us with joy.
> AMEN.

3rd Sunday of Easter   **Cycle A**

WE HAVE SEEN HIM

Things you need

Your Easter candle, matches, holy water, a bread roll or end of a loaf of bread.

Prepare your Bible

New Testament: St Luke, ch. 24, vv. 13-35.

To begin

Light your candle. Offer each other holy water. Sing "Alleluia" if you know any version, or a verse of an Easter hymn.

Leader   Lord Jesus, explain the scriptures to us.
            Make our hearts burn within us as you talk to us.
            Alleluia.

Gospel Reading

Choose one of the family to read the part of Jesus, two people for the disciples and a narrator who will also read the part of the Eleven. Try to start reading in the garden and come into the kitchen or dining room where you have put a plate with the bread on it. When the person reading the part of Jesus, takes the bread to bless it, he could say the prayer from the Offertory of the Mass which is an old Jewish blessing.

> "Blessed are you, Lord God of all creation,
> through your goodness we have this bread
> which earth has given and human hands have made".

c

Why do you think the two disciples did not recognise Jesus as he walked along beside them and spoke to them?

How can we tell that the crucifixion of Jesus had caused a great stir in Jerusalem?

How would you describe the mood of the two disciples?

How did they eventually recognise Jesus?

At what speed do you think they went back to Jerusalem?

Something to do

Play your happiest record or tape to express the mood of the disciples.

THE LORD IS MY SHEPHERD

Prepare your Bible

Old Testament: Psalm 22 (23)
　　　　The Lord is my Shepherd
New Testament: St. John, ch. 10,
　　　　　　　　vv. 1-10.

Your own experience

Remind each other of the times you have seen a flock of sheep, a shepherd, a sheepdog.

Responsorial Psalm 22 (23)

David was a shepherd boy before he became King. Shepherding was a well known occupation by the Jews. Here are a few facts about the habits of sheep. Find out in the psalm how David showed his knowledge of sheep behaviour.

　　1. The shepherd is responsible for finding grazing for his flock.
　　2. Sheep will not drink running water. The shepherd has to dam a stream to make a still pool.

34

3. The shepherd often goes ahead to cut down any plants which are poisonous to sheep so that they will wither in the sun before the flock arrives.

4. Each night the shepherd examines his sheep for cuts and sores and puts ointment on them.

Gospel Reading

Read the passage from St John and find out how Jesus is telling us the way he cares for us and knows us all.

Prayer

Father, eternal shepherd,
watch over the flock redeemed by the blood of Christ
and lead us to the promised land.
Bless our Bishop ...., and all the priests of our diocese.

5th Sunday of Easter   *Cycle A*

WE DEPEND ON JESUS

Things you need

Your Easter candle with flowers, matches. Leggo or building bricks if you have them.

Prepare your Bible

New Testament: 1 Peter, ch. 2, vv. 4-9;
                   St John, ch. 14, vv. 1-12.

First Reading

What is a cornerstone? What is a keystone? Can you demonstrate these two things with Leggo or bricks? Now read what St Peter says. If Peter's picture shows how we Christians are living stones built together with Jesus as our cornerstone or keystone, what happens if he is taken away? Show your model. What title does St Peter give to Christians?

Gospel Reading

Choose a narrator and someone to read the part of Jesus, Thomas and Philip.

What house is John referring to with its many rooms?

How are we to get there safely?

What phrase does Jesus use to show that he is as essential to us as the "cornerstone example" of Peter?

Prayer

Make up a prayer together by completing the phrases:—

Lord Jesus, you are the Way, help us to . . .

Lord Jesus, you are the Truth, help us to. . .

Lord Jesus, you are the Life, help us to . . .

When you have decided on your responses, pray it like a litany.

6th Sunday of Easter   *Cycle A*

JOY IN BELIEVING

Things you need

Your Easter candle with flowers, matches. A card with the word JOY written on it and decorated if possible. Paper and pencil.

Prepare your Bible

New Testament: Acts, ch. 8, vv. 5-8, 14-17;
                       St John, ch. 14, vv. 15-21.

Some phrases from the Mass

Speak out with a voice of joy.

Everliving God, help us to celebrate our joy . . .

Cry out with joy to God all the earth.

What natural things in the world give you joy? Notice at Mass the most joyous person you see, someone expressing joy by what they are wearing, the most joyful hymn you sing, the way the person who arranged the flowers has expressed her joy.

First Reading

On the 3rd Sunday of Lent, we saw how Jesus gave hope and joy to the Samaritan woman at the well. Now read today's event in Samaria. Why were the people filled with joy? How do you think they showed it? Why did Peter and John go to these new converts?

Gospel Reading

This is part of Jesus' farewell talk and prayer with his friends before his death. They did not understand what he meant but they trusted Jesus and knew he would keep his promise.

Write down the promise Jesus made:—

I shall ask the Father and he will . . .
I will not . . .
I will come . . .
On that day you will . . .

What is an advocate? Who is Jesus referring to?

Something to do

Try to leave your candle with your card of 'JOY' near it. Put the copies of the promises Jesus made somewhere where you can see them next week. You could use them as a prayer by saying each promise and adding, "Lord, I believe you".

7th Sunday of Easter　　　　　　　　　　　　　　　　**Cycle A**

PRAYER AND PRAISE

Things you need (if you have young children)

A cardboard box made into a flat-roofed house (sweet shops often have suitable boxes). Cut small windows and a doorway. Make steps up one side of the house leading to a door on the upper floor. Push a piece of cardboard inside the house to make the floor. Make about 15 figures out of paper or pipe cleaners.

Prepare your Bible

New Testament: Acts, ch. 1, vv. 12-14;
      St John, ch. 17, vv. 1-11.

First Reading

When you have read this, write the names of the people who are mentioned on the figures you have made. Put them in the upper room of your house. "They joined in continuous prayer".

— How do you think they did this? By singing? By reciting psalms? In silence? By reminding each other of the things Jesus had said to them?

— Here is a verse from the Responsorial Psalm on Sunday:
    The Lord is my light and my help;
    whom shall I fear?
    The Lord is the stronghold of my life;
    before whom shall I be afraid?

What special meaning would it have had for this group of people in the upper room?

Gospel Reading

This is part of Our Lord's prayer to his Father before he went out to his capture and death.

These words could well have been some of those which the disciples remembered in the upper room.

Listen, with your eyes closed, to your reader . . .

Keep quiet for a few moments after he has finished.

Prayer

    Leader—Jesus said: Eternal life is this,
      to know you, the only true God
      and Jesus Christ whom you have sent.
      (pause)

    Leader—Jesus said: I pray for them, Father,
      because they belong to you.
      (pause)

    Leader—Jesus said: All I have is yours, Father,
      and all you have is mine.
      (pause)

All   Glory be to the Father, and to the Son, and to the Holy Spirit, as it was in the beginning, is now and ever shall be, world without end. Amen.

Pentecost   *Cycle A, B, C*

COME, HOLY SPIRIT

Things you need

The house you made last week. A special cake for tea with a candle if possible. A map of the world or a globe. A tiny flag marked ALLELUIA on a pin. These gifts of the Holy Spirit written on small pieces of paper — peace, joy, forgiveness, love.

Prepare your Bible

New Testament: Acts, ch. 2, vv. 1-11;
                          St John, ch. 20, vv. 19-23.

First Reading

Put your house in the middle of the table where you are working. Pin your ALLELUIA flag on to the spot on your map or globe to mark Jerusalem.

As you read the text, bring your disciples out of the house at verse 4.

Frightened men had become brave. Nervous men had become confident. They had allowed the Holy Spirit to take over their lives.

A Prayer for us

      Come, Holy Spirit, fill our hearts with love.

Gospel Reading

Read how Jesus gave his apostles the Holy Spirit on Easter Day in the evening. What power was he giving his priests? Now look at the words you prepared. Talk about the way we receive these gifts each time we go to Confession.

(The birthday cake)	Here is a part of the Preface of the Mass on Whit Sunday: —
(Light the candle)	Today we celebrate the great beginning of your Church when the Holy Spirit made known to all people the one true God, and created from the many languages of man one voice to proclaim one faith.
(Put your flag on your cake)	The joy of the resurrection renews the whole world while the choirs of heaven sing for ever to your glory:
All	Holy, holy, holy Lord, God of power and might . . .

Sunday after Pentecost Cycle A, B, C

TRINITY SUNDAY

Things you need

A quiet room where everyone can sit comfortably and still. You may like to light a candle if this helps to bring stillness.

Leader — Tomorrow is Trinity Sunday. Let us start our preparation by showing that we belong to God.

All — In the name of the Father, and of the Son, and of the Holy Spirit.

Leader — A mystery is something that is true but which we cannot understand. The mystery of the Holy Trinity is the deepest mystery there is. *We* only know it because God has *revealed* it to us. Let us thank him for giving us the *faith* to believe.

All — Glory be to the Father and to the Son and to the Holy Spirit, as it was in the beginning, is now, and ever shall be, world without end. Amen

Leader — The Holy Trinity is a mystery of love — a mystery of perfect friendship — and the Holy Trinity dwells in each of us (pause).

40

Leader — We were baptised —

All — In the name of the Father, and of the Son, and of the Holy Spirit.

Leader — We were confirmed and we received forgiveness of our sins —

All — In the name of the Father, and of the Son, and of the Holy Spirit.

Leader — When we come to die, the Church will commend us to God by appealing to our faith —

All — In the name of the Father, and of the Son, and of the Holy Spirit.

Leader — With the sign of the cross we begin our prayer and our work —

All — In the name of the Father, and of the Son, and of the Holy Spirit.

Leader Here is the Preface of the Mass for Trinity Sunday:

We joyfully proclaim our faith
in the mystery of your Godhead.
You have revealed your glory
as the glory also of your Son
and of the Holy Spirit:
three Persons equal in majesty,
undivided in splendour,
yet one Lord, one God,
ever to be adored in your everlasting glory.

And so, with all the choirs of angels in heaven
we proclaim your glory
and join in their unending hymn of praise:

All (kneeling) Holy, holy, holy Lord, God of power and might,
heaven and earth are full of your glory.
Hosanna in the highest.
Blessed is he who comes in the name of the Lord.
Hosanna in the highest.

(stand) In the name of the Father, and of the Son, and of the Holy Spirit. AMEN.

HERE I AM

Prepare your Bible
Old Testament: Psalm 39 (40).

Introduction
The Book of Psalms which we find in our Bible is a collection of hymns and poems which the Jews used for their worship in the Temple. The psalms were written over a space of many centuries and they express the mood of the people who were going to sing them on different occasions. Sometimes they express joy, sometimes sadness and despair; sometimes they describe victory and triumph, sometimes even hatred and a plea to God to destroy their enemies.

In the Mass
We say or sing a psalm after the first reading and this has a response so that everyone can join in. That is why it is called a Responsorial Psalm. It is meant to help us to meditate on what God is saying to us through the scriptures.

The response to this Sunday's psalm is:
     Here I am, Lord!
     I come to do your will.

Think about yourself
Who am I? How old am I? What is my job at the moment? How can I do God's will in it? How can I know what God wants me to do?

First verse — I waited, I waited for the Lord
     and he stooped down to me; he heard my cry.
     He put a new song in my mouth, praise of our God.
     (What do you think made the psalmist write that?)

Second verse — You do not ask for sacrifice and offerings,
     but an open ear.
     You do not ask for holocausts and victims.
     Instead, here I am.
     (Do you understand all these words?
     How can we have "an open ear"?)

Third verse — In the scroll of the book it stands written
that I should do your will.
My God, I delight in your law in the depths of my heart.
(What, for us, is the "scroll of the book?")

To consider — How often do we pray: Thy will be done on earth as
it is in heaven — and really mean what we say?

JESUS — LIGHT OF THE WORLD

Things you need
Some pictures of people smiling.

Prepare your Bible
Isaiah, ch. 8, v. 23 to ch. 9, v. 3.

Text

"The people that walked in darkness
    has seen a great light;
on those who live in a land of deep
    shadow a light has shone".

Your experience
Think of some occasions when you have been in darkness and then
suddenly a light has come: e.g., after a fuse or an electricity cut, in
the garage before the car headlights go on.

Have you ever been in a tunnel, moving towards the light?

Do you know anyone who has had an eye operation? What did they
feel like when the bandages were removed?

From the Mass

Response to the psalm: The Lord is my light and my help.

Communion antiphon: Look up at the Lord with gladness
    and smile.

Discuss

In the dark, things have no shape, we fall over, we can get hurt, we cannot see where to go.

How is this true for people who do not know Jesus Christ?

Smile please

Look at the pictures you found. How a smile lights up a face!

At the moment of the consecration at Mass, when the priest says: THIS IS MY BODY, and holds up the Host for us to adore, let us smile in our hearts at Jesus Christ present among us.

When we come to the Sign of Peace, let us smile at the people with whom we exchange it. Jesus Christ is present in us all.

4th Sunday of the Year   *Cycle A*

HOW TO BE HAPPY!

Things you need

A picture of St Bernadette, or St Thérèse of Lisieux, or St Martin de Porres, or Pope John XXIII or St John Bosco. A photo of your family showing as many members as possible (a wedding often gathers a family together).

Prepare your Bible

Old Testament: Zephaniah, ch. 2, v. 3; ch. 3, vv. 12-13.
New Testament: 1 Corinthians, ch. 1, vv. 26-31;
                 St Matthew, ch. 5, vv. 1-12.

First Reading

What is the key word in this passage from Zephaniah?
What is the phrase which shows how happy God's people will be?

Second Reading

How does this picture link up with the saint whose picture you have found?

Look at your own family photo. Each one is called and chosen by God. Some members may be doing a very special work for God's family.

"God has made you members of Christ Jesus". When did this happen ?

Prayer

Lord our God,
help us to love you with all our hearts
and to love all men as you love them,
through Christ our Lord. Amen.

Gospel Reading

This is part of the "Sermon on the Mount". Can you see from verse 1, why it has been given this name. Sometimes it is called "The Beatitudes". Can you see why this is another description of this particular teaching of Jesus?

Take one or two verses that you specially like and think about them together. The person preparing this week's study should have some ideas ready; for example, "Happy the gentle — they shall have the earth for their heritage".

Who do you know who has a gentle voice, a gentle smile, gentle hands, a gentle way with animals . . .? Gentle people respect others — they don't push to have their own way or to be first in a queue. Gentleness leads to friendliness and trust. Jesus asks his followers to be gentle.

5th Sunday of the Year　　　　　　　　　　　　　　　　　**Cycle A**

SHINE IN THE DARK

Things you need

Pencil and paper. Candle and matches. A bucket (not plastic).

Prepare your Bible

Old Testament: Isaiah, ch. 58, vv. 7-10.
New Testament: St Matthew, ch. 5, vv. 13-16.

Introduction

At Christmas time we think of Christ as light of the world and the Sunday before last we were thinking how a smile can "light up" our faces.

Because we are members of the Church — the people of God — part of Christ's body, the Church — we have to let the light of Christ shine through us.

First Reading

Read this passage together and then write down six things. God says: this: Your light will shine like the dawn if:—

        a)

        b)

        c)

        d)

God says this: Your light will rise in the darkness and your shadows become like noon if:—

        a) You do away with . . .

        b) If you give . . .

Gospel Reading

Read these words of Jesus and see how all the good and kind and thoughtful and unselfish things we do, give praise to our Father in heaven.

Experiment

See if you can illustrate the example that Jesus gave.

Light your candle and put in the middle of the table. Cover it with the bucket (not plastic, remember!).

1st speaker: No one lights a lamp to put it under a tub.

2nd speaker: (lifting off the bucket) They put it on the lamp stand where it shines for everyone in the house.

46

Prayer

Sit quietly for a moment and think how you can shine with love, happiness, peace, kindness.

> "Brighten, I pray thee, my Jesus,
> brighten my lamp with your light".

(Prayer of St Columbanus)

6th Sunday of the Year   **Cycle A**

THE LAW OF LOVE

Things you need

A few examples of rules and regulations, e.g., Highway Code, Guide or Scout Law, instructions for using a machine, school rules, etc.

Prepare your Bible

Old Testament: Ecclesiasticus, ch. 15, vv. 15-20.
New Testament: St Matthew, ch. 5, vv. 17-37.

Opening Prayer

> God our Father,
> you have promised to remain for ever
> with those who do what is just and right.
> Help us to live in your presence.

Discussion

Look at the rules and codes you have found. Decide which ones are made for our safety, for our happiness, for the comfort of other people. Do you ever have to *choose* whether to follow the rule?

First Reading

Read the passage. What are the commandments that are referred to? How can you tell that we are free to choose how we live? How can you tell that we *are able* to live in God's way?

Introduction to the Gospel

Over hundreds of years, the Jews were learning to know God and how to live in his way. Gradually their leaders built up so many rules and regulations that it was impossible to keep them all. Jesus was brought up as a Jew by Our Lady and St Joseph. He had been to school and had been taught the Law by the Jewish teachers called rabbis. Now read the Gospel.

Jesus goes further

Jesus wasn't going to do away with God's important Laws (The Ten Commandments) but he was going to show men how to keep them more faithfully. He did not add to the Laws but went to the heart of them, thus giving new life.

Some examples

You know you mustn't kill. What did Jesus say?

If you are going to worship God and you remember you are not at peace with your brother, what must you do?

You know you mustn't swear. What is it enough to say?

At Mass

The Sign of Peace at Mass is the kind of moment Jesus is thinking about. When we shake hands, it is a *sign* that we want to be at peace with *everyone*.

7th Sunday of the Year   *Cycle A*

TIT FOR TAT? NO!

What you need

A crucifix that everyone can see (or a picture).

Prepare your Bible

New Testament: St Matthew, ch. 6, vv. 38-48.

Opening prayer — (To ask God to make us more like his Son.)

> Father,
> keep before us the wisdom and love
> you have revealed in your Son.
> Help us to be like him
> in word and deed
> for he lives and reigns with you and the Holy Spirit,
> one God, for ever and ever.
> Amen.

Gospel Reading

If we are to be more like Jesus Christ, we must try to know him better. The Gospel today tells us the kind of things Jesus expects his followers to be able to do *with his help.*

Read the passage slowly and thoughtfully.

— What do you think of letting someone hit you twice?
— What about handing over your raincoat when someone has already borrowed your blazer?
— What about going double the distance you have been told to go?
— What about giving to anyone who asks for something and always being ready to lend your things?

Jesus expects Christians to have very high standards: "to be perfect as our heavenly Father is perfect". We know we can't manage alone — only by letting Jesus Christ come into our lives and letting him live in us can we gradually become "other Christs".

Looking at your crucifix

In giving his life for us, Jesus gave up everything because he loved us. What an example of perfect love!

Here is the prayer after Communion. If we say 'Amen', we must really mean it.

> Almighty God,
> help us to live the example of love
> we celebrate in this Eucharist,
> that we may come to its fulfilment
> in your presence.

D

THE TREMENDOUS LOVE OF GOD

Things you need

A picture or photo of a mother with a very small baby; a picture of some birds and one of some flowers.

Prepare your Bible

Old Testament: Isaiah, ch. 49, vv. 14-15 (if you wish).
New Testament: St Matthew, ch. 6, vv. 24-34.

First Reading

In the first reading today, the prophet Isaiah is telling the people who are in trouble and who are afraid that God has abandoned them, that God says this:

> "Does a woman forget her baby at the breast,
> or fail to cherish the son of her womb?
> Yet even if these forget,
> I will never forget you".

Look at your picture of the mother with her baby. What signs can you see of her love and care? Ask your mother how often she used to feed you when you were a tiny baby. How long did each feed take? If she made a bottle for you, how did she do it?

To show how much God loves us, Isaiah tried to choose an example of the greatest love and care in the world.

Gospel Reading

Have your two other pictures ready and read the passage.

What is the most common bird around your house? Perhaps a sparrow or starling — or gull if you live by the sea. Have you ever seen a flock of birds flying across the sky at night?

Have you ever found a dead bird? How did you think it died? Have you a bird table? Do you put out water for the birds in winter?

Look at your picture of a flower. Have you a living flower in your home at the moment?

Jesus says that not even the great and rich King Solomon had clothes as beautiful as the various flowers that grow in our fields and gardens.

And who provides nourishment for them all? . . .

Prayer

Thank God for his goodness in a prayer or in a hymn such as:
  "All things bright and beautiful . . ."

9th Sunday of the Year   *Cycle A*

OUR GOD FOR EVER AND EVER

Things you need

Write neatly on four pieces of paper, "You must love the Lord your God with all your heart, with all your soul, with all your strength." Find two pieces of ribbon or tape (string would do). A small piece of sellotape. An empty matchbox or other small box.

Prepare your Bible

Old Testament: Deuteronomy, ch. 11, vv. 18-21, 26-28.
New Testament: St Matthew, ch. 7, vv. 21-27.

First Reading

Read the passage and then fasten one of your pieces of paper on the left wrist with ribbon or tape. Fold a second text, put it in the matchbox and tie it on your forehead with the tape going right round your head. This is like a phylactery worn by the Jews. Read verses 19-21 and decide where you will put your other two copies of the text. Why did Moses tell his people to do this? vv. 21, 27.

Gospel Reading

Read Our Lord's words to his disciples and the story he told. Jesus is telling them that it is no good just *saying* that we love God. We have *to do* what he wants.

— What does this mean today for each of us? — a chance to help

someone, leaving time for our prayers, something we know we ought to do today but that we have been putting off?
— We have to listen to what Jesus teaches and rely on him.

You could act this (if you have young children)

Let Dad or a strong brother be the house built first on rock and then on sand. Recite the word together as you act it out.

Rains came down, floods rose,
gales blew and hurled themselves against that house,
AND IT DID NOT FALL. It was founded on rock.

Rains came, floods rose,
gales blew and struck that house,
AND IT FELL, and what a fall it had!

Restore calm to the family and talk about dangers that can hit a family
— illness, poverty, redundancy . . .

Prayer

Leader   Father,
          your love never fails.
          Hear our call.
          Keep us from danger
          and provide for all our needs.
          We make our prayer through Christ our Lord. Amen.

10th Sunday of the Year   **Cycle A**

SHOWING OUR LOVE

Things you need

A present you made for your mother or father when you were very young, e.g., mat, picture, clay dish, etc.

Prepare your Bible

Old Testament: Hosea, ch. 6, vv. 3-6.
New Testament: St Matthew, ch. 9, vv. 9-13.

First Reading

Hosea is contrasting God's faithful love for us with our changeable love for him.

What three word pictures does Hosea paint to describe the certainty of God's coming to us?

What two things does he use to describe the way our love for God often disappears so quickly?

What are the two things God wants from us?

Gospel Reading

God calls each one of us. Read how Jesus called Matthew. How did Matthew celebrate his joy in becoming a follower of Jesus?

What did Jesus mean when he said: "It is not the healthy who need the doctor but the sick. I did not come to call the virtuous but sinners".

To talk about

Look at the present you found. Can you remember making it? Did it take a long time to make? Were you pleased with your efforts? How did your mother or father feel about it? Did it matter to her how much money, if any, it cost? What really mattered?

Prayer

Here is the prayer the priest will say at Mass to offer our gifts to God:

Look with love on our service.
Accept the gifts we bring
and help us to grow in Christian love.

Final thought

God said: What I want is love, not sacrifice.
Jesus said: What I want is mercy, not sacrifice.

Sacrifice here means the offering of animals to be killed and burnt to give honour to God. What does God want from us instead of this old way to give him honour?

YOU SHALL BE MY VERY OWN

Things you need

Draw a picture of tents pitched at the foot of a mountain. Write on a card the word COVENANT.

Prepare your Bible

Old Testament: Exodus, ch. 19, vv. 2-6.
New Testament: St Matthew, ch. 9, v. 36; ch. 10, v. 8.

First Reading

— What had God done with the Egyptians? (See Exodus, ch. 14, if you are not sure.)

— Why did God choose to describe the way he helped the Israelites as "carrying you on eagles' wings"?

— "I will count you a kingdom of priests, a consecrated nation".

Do you know anyone who is consecrated?

Do you know any object that is consecrated?

What do you mean by "the consecration" during Mass?

Gospel Reading

This passage is often chosen when we are praying especially for vocations to the priesthood and to religious life.

— What sort of harvest does Jesus mean?

— Jesus gave his disciples certain authority. In which *sacraments* do our bishops and priests use this authority today?

Consider together

"You received without charge, give without charge". These words are for us too. Let us think of some of the things God has given us without charge — health, talents, possessions . . .

How can we give "without charge?"

> Almighty God,
> our hope and strength,
> without you we falter.
> Help us to follow Christ
> and to live according to your will.
> We ask this through Christ Our Lord.
> Amen.

12th Sunday of the Year   **Cycle A**

SAFE WITH GOD

Things you need
Two pieces of paper or card; felt tip pens or crayons.

Prepare your Bible
Old Testament: Jeremiah, ch. 20, vv. 10-13.
New Testament: St Matthew, ch. 10, vv. 26-33.

First Reading
Jeremiah was a peaceful man but God used him to warn his people of coming strife and disaster. This made him unpopular and he barely escaped death. Sometimes he was tempted to give up proclaiming God's message. Read how his friends deserted him. See how he trusted in God.

Gospel Reading
Jesus had often taught his disciples when they were alone with him, but his message, his Good News, was to be proclaimed by them to everyone. This could bring them into danger.
— How does Jesus assure his disciples that God the Father will take care of them?
— Have we a duty to let other people see that we believe in God?

Something to do

Make two posters of SMILE GOD LOVES YOU or GOD IS LOVE or any other Christian slogan you like at the moment. Put the posters you have made (or a picture or statue if you prefer) near your front and back door so that everyone who comes to your house will know that you are a Christian family.

13th Sunday of the Year   *Cycle A*

WELCOME!

Things you need
A card or piece of paper, felt tips or crayons.

Prepare your Bible
Old Testament: 2 Kings, ch. 4, vv. 8-16.
New Testament: St Matthew, ch. 10, vv. 37-42.

First Reading
— How did Elisha's friendship with the lady and her husband develop?
— Elisha wanted to repay them in some way. What did his servant Gehazi suggest?

Gospel Reading
In the Gospel, Jesus is showing us how our love for him must be the first love of our life. It does not exclude loving other people, but it must come first. Our love for other people leads us to Jesus very often. What does Jesus say about welcoming him?

To talk about
— How do we welcome people who come to our house? Those who come to tea, to stay the night, to collect for charity, to borrow something, etc. How do we answer the 'phone?

— How do we welcome Jesus Christ in Holy Communion?
Do we get ready to receive him? Do we talk to him and listen to him?

Something to do

Make a card saying WELCOME and put it in your window or by your door. You could put it beside the card you made last week.

14th Sunday of the Year   *Cycle A*

THE KINDNESS OF GOD

Things you need (if you have young children in your family).

A tray with small objects covered by a cloth or a closed tin with something inside.

Prepare your Bible

Old Testament: Zechariah, ch. 9, vv. 9-10.
New Testament: St Matthew, ch. 11, vv. 25-30.

First Reading

This will probably remind you of Palm Sunday. It is one of the passages of scripture, written about 520 years before Christ, that the disciples may have remembered when Jesus entered Jerusalem.
— What phrases in this reading show that the Messiah was going to bring peace?

Gospel Reading

Sometimes we think that because God is so great and powerful and full of wisdom, we are not able to understand him at all. We cannot find out everything about him by using our minds, but God "reveals" himself to us in various ways.
— Ask your family what is under the cloth covering your tray. They won't be able to say. Take off the cloth and "reveal" what you have prepared.

— Read the Gospel.

vv. 25-27. To whom does Jesus reveal the Good News of God? Generally, oxen and bullocks are yoked together so that they can share the weight they are pulling. Jesus and St Joseph probably made wooden yokes to sell to local farmers.

— Read vv. 28-30. How does Jesus show that he wants to help us?

— How can we tell that following Jesus may involve hardship?

15th Sunday of the Year   *Cycle A*

GROWING

Things you need

The lid of a tin or box filled with soil. Make a path across it with stones. Put a big stone to look like a rock and some prickly, thorny twigs in one corner.

Prepare your Bible

Old Testament: Isaiah, ch. 55, vv. 10-11;
Psalm 64 (65), vv. 9-13 (You care for the earth . . .).
New Testament: St Matthew, ch. 13, vv. 1-9, 18-23.

First Reading

What picture does Isaiah use to show that God's message always reaches its destination?

Responsorial Psalm

You are probably preparing this Mass on a lovely summer day. Read the psalm and then think what signs you have seen around you of —

— the earth filled with riches.
— the first fruits of the earth.
— the hillsides wrapped with joy.
— meadows covered with flocks.
— valleys clothed with wheat.

Gospel Reading

As you read this passage, look at the "field" you have prepared. Jesus was talking about people. The seed of his life is sown in us when we are baptised. We have to see that the soil in which the seed grows is good soil. What have parents and godparents promised to do with our "soil?"

Prayer

Let us ask God to make us good soil so that we may receive his word and let it grow in us:

Lord,
accept the gifts of your Church.
May this Eucharist
help us to grow in holiness and faith.
Lord, by our sharing in the mystery of this Eucharist,
let your saving love grow within us.

16th Sunday of the Year   *Cycle A*

GOD'S PATIENCE

Prepare your Bible

Old Testament: Wisdom, ch. 12, vv. 13, 16-19..
                        Psalm 85 (86), vv. 5, 6, 9, 10. 15, 16 (Lord, you
                        are good and forgiving).
New Testament: St Matthew, ch. 13, vv. 24-30.

First Reading

Most of the gods surrounding the Chosen People only belonged to a tribe or a certain country. What was so special about God, the true God?

— By God's lenience towards us, what must we understand about our dealings with one another?

— What is the great and sure hope that we, as God's children, may have of our heavenly Father?

If we had only this description of our God, would it be sufficient to tell the unbelievers about him?

Gospel Reading

A parable is a story with a hidden meaning and it was one of the favourite ways Jesus used to teach his disciples.

Darnel or tares looked very much like wheat when young and the seeds of the tare mixed with corn could make the eater ill. It was difficult to sow "clean" seed in a field and however much care was taken, an evil-minded man could come when it was dark and scatter tare-seed in a neighbour's field of corn.

— Read the parable. Why did the farmer prevent his servants from going out and trying to weed out the darnel or tares?

— This parable is about the kingdom of heaven. What does it tell us about the people who live in God's kingdom? Does God "weed us out" impatiently?

What does Jesus mean by "harvest time?"

Now you could read vv. 36-43.

Prayer

Let us pray to be kept faithful in the service of God.
Lord, be merciful to your people.
Fill us with your gifts
and make us always eager to serve you
in faith, hope and love.

17th Sunday of the Year   *Cycle A*

A PRECIOUS GIFT

Things you need

A pearl necklace or another piece of jewelry containing a pearl if you can borrow it. Do you know how pearls are made?

Prepare your Bible

Old Testament: 1 Kings, ch. 3, vv. 5, 7-12.
New Testament: St Matthew, ch. 13, vv. 44-52.

First Reading

Read the passage together.

— Who was Solomon's father?
— Who were the people he had to rule?
— How would you describe Solomon's character?
— Some people today have the custom when they go into church for the very first time, of asking God for three "graces". (This is much more serious than wishing when we cut a birthday cake or when we pull the wishbone of a chicken or turkey!) What do you think of Solomon's "grace" which was "give your servant a heart to understand how to discern good and evil"?

Gospel Reading

You remember that a parable is a story with a hidden meaning. Here it contains a lesson for us. We have three stories to help us to understand the kingdom of heaven.

— vv. 44-46. What are these two stories meant to tell us?
Can you think of anyone who has done this?
— vv. 47-50. If you have ever gone shrimping, you know how your net collects everything in it and you have to sort out the shrimps from the seaweed, etc. How does this parable compare with the one we read last Sunday?
— vv. 51, 52. Scribes were experts on the Jewish Law and so those who followed Jesus and became his disciples were able to draw on their store of Old Testament learning as well as on the things they learned anew from Jesus.

Prayer

Let us pray that we will make good use of the gifts
that God has given us.

God our Father and protector,
without you nothing is holy,
nothing has value.
Guide us to everlasting life.
by helping us to use wisely
the blessings you have given to the world.

GOD'S CARE FOR US

Things you need
A picture which reminds you
of Holy Communion.

Prepare your Bible
Old Testament: Isaiah, ch. 55, vv. 1-3.
New Testament:
     Romans, ch. 55, vv. 1-3.
     St Matthew, ch. 14, vv. 13-21.

First Reading
This part of the book of Isaiah was written while the people of God
were still in exile. These verses form part of the prophecy that
Jerusalem will once again be restored to the exiles.
— What picture in words does the writer use to show the happiness
     that is in store for these people?
— v. 2. Is good food and drink the only thing necessary for happiness?
— v. 3. What is the "everlasting covenant" for us?
     Think of the words of consecration at Mass.

Second Reading
Read these lovely words slowly. After a short pause to think about
them, read them again.

Gospel Reading
We call this miracle one of the "figures" or "types" of the Holy
Eucharist. This means that the action of Jesus in feeding these hungry
people who stayed with him all day because they wanted to be near
him and to listen to him, was an advance preparation for the Eucharist.
— Why do you think Jesus wanted his disciples to come away with
     him?
— When his plan was spoiled, did Jesus show he was put out?
— v. 15. What does this tell us about the way Jesus spoke to people?

— v. 19. How do the actions of Jesus compare with the actions of a priest saying Mass at the moment of consecration?

— Jesus wanted the disciples to give the people food and he gave them the power to do this. How is the same power used by the priests today to make sure that God's people have the food they need so that God's life in them can grow?

The opening prayer of the Mass

Father of everlasting goodness,
our origin and guide,
be close to us
and hear the prayers of all who praise you.
Forgive our sins and restore us to life.
Keep us safe in your love.

19th Sunday of the Year   *Cycle A*

PEACE WITH GOD

Things you need

Pictures of a rough and a calm sea. You might have a record with music which begins loudly and becomes soft and gentle. (Pastoral Symphony by Beethoven.)

Prepare your Bible

Old Testament: 1 Kings, ch. 19, vv. 9, 11-13.
New Testament: St Matthew, ch. 14, vv. 22-33.

First Reading

Elijah was spending the night in a cave because his life was in danger and he was hiding. The Children of Israel had turned away from God and wanted to kill Elijah because he continued faithful to God in spite of everything.

— In what signs of power did Elijah expect to meet God?

— What was the sign that God chose?

— What did Elijah do when he realised that he was in the presence of God? Is there a time when we bow our heads in the presence of God? (Think of Mass.)

Gospel Reading

— Has any member of your family an experience of a storm at sea? Would they share the experience so that the rest can understand what they felt like?

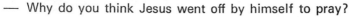

— Read the passage which follows on last week's Gospel.

— Why do you think Jesus went off by himself to pray?

— The fourth watch of the night is between 3 and 6 a.m. vv. 24, 25. How long does it seem the disciples were struggling with the storm?

— vv. 27, 28. What did Jesus say? Can you think of an occasion in our own lives when we might call to Jesus for help and these words would help us?

— v. 33. Like Elijah when he recognised the presence of God, these fishermen bowed down before Jesus. What did they say?

Act of faith from the Creed we say at Mass.

> We believe in one Lord Jesus Christ,
> the only Son of God.

20th Sunday of the Year   *Cycle A*

GOD IS FOR EVERYONE

Things you need

Cut out all the pictures of people in a newspaper or a magazine. Arrange them on your table round your Bible or round a lighted candle.

Prepare your Bible

Old Testament: Isaiah, ch. 56, vv. 1, 6-7.
New Testament: St Matthew, ch. 15, vv. 21-28.

First Reading

These verses were probably written after the People of God had returned from Exile. Perhaps foreigners had joined the Chosen People, the writer is explaining that they must be made welcome.

— v. 6. What must these foreigners agree to do?
— v. 7. How does the writer express God's desire for all men to know him and to worship him?

Gospel Reading

The woman in this episode was a pagan and yet she came to ask Jesus to heal her daughter.

— Why do you think Jesus seemed to ignore her at first?
— How can we tell that she was not put off by his attitude?
— Why did the disciples want Jesus to listen to her?
— v. 24. What did Jesus mean?
— v. 26. What did Jesus mean?
— v. 27. Why did this answer please Jesus?
— We are not told what happened after her daughter was cured. What do you think might have been the result?

Responsorial Psalm

Light your candle and look at the pictures you have prepared. Here are some verses from the psalm:

"Let the peoples praise you" — how many nationalities are represented in your pictures?

"Let your face shed its light upon us". Are there any of the people in special need of God's help?

"Let the nations be glad and exult for you rule the world with justice". Do any of your pictures show injustice? Could you pray for these people?

"May God still give us his blessing till the ends of the earth revere him". Let us ask God to bless all the people we have represented in our pictures.

E

WE BELIEVE

Things you need
A picture of St Peter and/or the Holy Father.

Prepare your Bible
Old Testament: Isaiah, ch. 22, vv. 19-23.
New Testament: Romans, ch. 11, vv. 33-36.
          St Matthew, ch. 16, vv. 13-20.

First Reading
This part of Isaiah was written when the prophet could predict the failure and downfall of the nation — but he could also foresee something more wonderful to come afterwards.
— What signs of authority were given to Eliakim?
— What kind of authority was he to exercise over Jerusalem?
— "I will drive him like a peg into a firm place". What does this picture tell us about his position?

Gospel Reading
Read this passage and then say why our Old Testament reading was chosen to go with it.
— Jesus created a problem for those who lived round him. He was such a wonderful person that people compared him with the prophets of the past and even thought he might be one of them come back again. What names were suggested?
— v. 17. This is sometimes called St Peter's confession of faith. How did Jesus say that Peter had arrived at this faith?
— All faith is a gift. When were we given this gift?
  Has our faith deepened over the years through progressive "revelation" — through people we have known? Through words of the Bible suddenly coming alive for us? During our prayer? . . .
— What verse seems to you to be like "the peg in a firm place"?
— v. 19. What does a key symbolise for you?
  This verse gives us the basis for all authority in the Church. Who is the successor of St Peter today?

Read these verses of St Paul slowly. After a few moments re-read them. Could each person say which phrase stays most clearly in his mind?

Prayer

> Merciful God,
> the perfect sacrifice of Jesus Christ
> made us your people.
> In your love,
> grant peace and unity to your Church.

22nd Sunday of the Year   ***Cycle A***

REAL LIFE

Things you need
A crucifix.

Prepare your Bible
Old Testament: Jeremiah, ch. 20, vv. 7-9.
New Testament: St Matthew, ch. 16, vv. 21-27.

First Reading
Jeremiah was a loving, gentle person who experienced great difficulty in being true to what he believed. He found that he had to be the mouthpiece announcing tragedy and doom for his country. These verses show how he could not resist God in spite of the suffering his loyalty brought him.

— How did people treat him?

— What seems to be the message perpetually on his lips? What would the people feel about someone who was always telling them disastrous news?

— v. 9. Why did Jeremiah find that he could not stop thinking about God and speaking for him?

Gospel Reading

Here we read how Jesus tried to break the news to his disciples that his life was not going to end in the obvious triumph and glory that they were expecting.

— How did Peter react to this?

— v. 23. Can you think of any times when you have realised that God's way of working in your life or in the life of someone you know, is not your way?

— v. 25. A very well known and important verse for a Christian. The word "life" here refers sometimes to life on this earth and sometimes to the eternal life to which we are looking forward. Re-read the verse and think about this.

If you know the stories of any martyrs, you can see how they gave up one life for the sake of gaining the other.

Blessing

May the Lord bless us,
may he keep us from all evil,
and lead us to life everlasting. Amen.

23rd Sunday of the Year   *Cycle A*

CORRECT ONE ANOTHER
WITH LOVE

Prepare your Bible

Old Testament: Ezekiel, ch. 33, vv. 7-9.
New Testament: St Matthew, ch. 18, vv. 15-20.

First Reading

— What is a sentry? Where have you seen a sentry posted? Where have you read about a sentry on guard?

— Ezekiel is another prophet who had to issue warnings on the part of God that trouble and disaster was to overtake the people. However, the verses we are reading are just beginning to introduce a more hopeful future.

— In these verses, what is the sentry's responsibility?
— If he carries out his responsibility but no one takes any notice, what will happen?

Response to the Psalm

O that today you would listen to his voice! Harden not your hearts.
— What does that mean?

Gospel Reading

Jesus knows that things can go wrong between people. If we really love someone, this may entail correcting him. Do you agree?
— In this passage Jesus is talking to his apostles — those who are to have the responsibility of his Church. How does Jesus tell them they must deal with people who do something wrong?
— v. 20. Read this verse again. Then think how it applies to you now.

Prayer

The Risen Jesus is present among you. Are there any special things for which you want to pray?

Motto for the week

Love is the one thing that cannot hurt your neighbour. (Listen for this sentence at Mass on Sunday.)

24th Sunday of the Year   *Cycle A*

FORGIVENESS

Things you need

Write out "Forgive us our trespasses as we forgive those who trespass against us".

Prepare your Bible

Old Testament: Ecclesiasticus, ch. 27, v. 30, ch. 28, v. 7.
New Testament: St Matthew, ch. 18, vv. 21-35.

First Reading

Here are the negative words in this passage: Resentment, anger, vengeance, nursing anger, show no pity, hating, ill-will.

— Can you explain to each other what these words mean?
— Here are the positive words: Forgive, compassion, overlook the offence.
— Can you add more words to this list which show a Christian outlook?

Response to the Psalm

> The Lord is compassion and love,
> slow to anger and rich in mercy.

Have you any relatives or friends who are outstanding in these Christian qualities?

Gospel Reading

Look at the sentence from the Lord's prayer that you have written out.

— We ask God our Father to forgive us in the same way as we forgive other people. Can we think for a few minutes about this?

Are we quick to forgive others?

> Can we forget the way we have been hurt by them?
>
> Can we start again after a quarrel and try to be friends?
>
> Do we make it easy for people to say sorry to us?

— Before you read the Gospel, do a little arithmetic. If one talent is worth about £300 and one denarius is worth about 1p., work out the sums of money involved. They are exaggerated deliberately to make the point of the story clear.

Now read the parable with the English money equivalent you have found. Talk about this.

Prayer from the Mass

> Almighty God,
> our creator and guide,
> may we serve you with all our heart
> and know your forgiveness in our lives. Amen.
> Forgive us our trespasses as we forgive those
> who trespass against us.

GENEROSITY

Things you need

A pile of six or seven one-penny pieces. Small cards with these
times written on them: 9 a.m., 12 noon, 3 p.m., 5 p.m.

Prepare your Bible

Old Testament: Isaiah, ch. 55, vv. 6-9.
New Testament: St Matthew, ch. 20, vv. 1-16.

First Reading

The readings today follow the thought we had last week of the immense
goodness and kindness and patience of God. Anyone who has turned
away from God is invited to turn back — to repent. How will he be
received by God?

— We cannot begin to understand God's ways. Very often he seems
   to forgive much more easily than we do. What words in this
   reading show that God's ways of working are so different from ours?

Gospel Reading

This parable which Jesus told was really meant to show that no one
is ever too late to come into God's kingdom. The Jews thought that
they would always be dearest to God because he had chosen them to
be his own people. Jesus came to show us that God loves all men no
matter what their race or belief, and that his love is more wonderful
than we can ever understand.

— Choose someone to read the part of the owner of the vineyard,
   someone to be the bailiff with the money and give a "time card"
   to four other people. Choose a narrator and read the Gospel
   together.

Something to discuss

Do we sometimes say, "It isn't fair"? Can we think of some occasions?
Do we sometimes say to God, "It isn't fair"?

          — Why has this happened to me?
          — Why was I made redundant?

— Why have I such a quick temper?

— Why isn't my hair curly?

Prayer over the gifts

We can offer to God our love and trust in spite of the difficult things in our life. His thoughts are above our thoughts and his ways are above our ways — AND HE LOVES US.

Lord,
may these gifts which we now offer
to show our belief and our love
be pleasing to you.
May they become for us
the eucharist of Jesus Christ your Son,
who is Lord for ever and ever. Amen.

26th Sunday of the Year   *Cycle A*

YES!

Things you need

Before you meet as a family, think of an occasion when someone has acted like the two sons in the Gospel. It could be a question of helping with the washing-up or going shopping or taking the dog for a walk or collecting on a flag day.

Prepare your Bible

New Testament:
Philippians, ch. 2, vv. 1-11.
St Matthew, ch. 21, vv. 28-32.

Gospel Reading

Tell your family the incident you have prepared and ask them if they can think of any other similar ones.

— Read the Gospel together. Jesus often said things to the officials of the Jewish religion that they did not like. Imagine being told that public sinners would be welcomed by God rather than themselves! Why? See v. 32.

First Reading

Read vv. 1-5 slowly and talk about each sentence that St Paul writes to the people of Philippi.
— What convictions do all Christians share?
— There is nothing that God asks us to do that he has not done himself. Read vv. 6-8. How does this assure us that Jesus has shared our human life?
— vv. 9-11. BUT . . . the passion and death of Jesus led to his glorious life. Stand up to read these last verses together.

Prayer said together:
Dying you destroyed our death,
Rising you restored our life,
LORD JESUS COME IN GLORY.

27th Sunday of the Year   *Cycle A*

THE VINEYARD OF THE LORD

Things you need

Prepare a plan or drawing of a field on a hillside (to catch the sun) with a wall and hedge round it. Don't forget a gate. Draw a watchtower in the middle with rows of vines. Show a hole near the tower where a wine press could be.

Prepare your Bible

Old Testament: Isaiah, ch. 5, vv. 1-7.
New Testament: St Matthew, ch. 21, vv. 33-43.

First Reading

— What steps did the owner of the vineyard take to ensure a good grape harvest?

— *But* what were the grapes like at harvest time?

— What did the owner think to himself?

— He was so disappointed — what did he do?

— Isaiah is comparing the People of God to the vines in this story, but we can take it as a story for the Church today.

— How does God take care of us so that we shall grow to be mature Christian men and women?

— We are "choice vines", precious and beautiful to God. How can we try to produce the sweet grapes he is expecting of us?

St Paul's answer

Fill your minds with everything that is true, everything that is noble, everything that is good and pure, everything that we love and honour, and everything that can be thought virtuous or worthy of praise. (Philippians, ch. 4, vv. 6-9.)

Gospel Reading

Here the artist explains his drawing to the family! Make sure everybody knows what a tenant is. Now read the Gospel — a terrible illustration of the way the Jews were going to treat the Son of God. Prophets had come to prepare the way for him — they had not been given a hearing. The last prophet, John the Baptist, had been beheaded. Jesus, the Son of God, was being rejected by the very people who, through knowledge of the scriptures, should have recognised him and welcomed him.

— To whom was Jesus was telling this parable? v. 33.

— What did Jesus mean by v. 43?

Prayer

Let us ask God to forgive us for the times we have failed to produce the fruit he was expecting and for the times we have refused to listen to his Son.

Father,
forgive our failings,
keep us in your peace
and lead us in the way of salvation.

74

GOD'S INVITATION

Things you need
A picture which will remind you of Holy Communion.

Prepare your Bible
Old Testament: Isaiah, ch. 25, vv. 1-14.
New Testament: St Matthew, ch. 22, vv. 1-14.

First Reading
— What word is used for a meal?
— What is your idea of this kind of meal?
— For whom is this banquet prepared? What is going to be eaten?
— This is an attempt to describe heaven. How does Isaiah try to explain the happiness that awaits us all?

Gospel Reading
This is another parable that Jesus told to the chief priests and elders. He seemed to want to give them every chance to understand his message.
— Why had the king arranged a feast?
— What had he prepared for the meal?
— How can we tell that he was really anxious that those invited should come? (Who was Jesus thinking of?)
— Who attended the wedding feast in the end? How can we tell that God wants everyone to know him and to be happy with him for ever?
— What are the words the priest says to invite us to Holy Communion, as he shows us the Host?

Responsorial Psalm
The response to the psalm is:
　　　　　In the Lord's own house shall I dwell for ever and ever.
— We often call our church — God's house. Here we are always welcome. Here we come to be fed at the Lord's table. What will be our eternal dwelling place?

Prayer

Put your picture where everyone can see it, and say this prayer slowly:

This is a holy banquet indeed,
in which Christ himself is made our food;
the memory of his Passion is told again;
grace fills our mind and heart;
and there is given to us an assurance
of the glory that will one day be ours.

29th Sunday of the Year   **Cycle A**

KING OF MY LIFE

Things you need
A variety of coins including foreign ones if possible.

Prepare your Bible
Old Testament: Psalm 95 (96) O sing a new song to the Lord.
New Testament: St Matthew, ch. 22, vv. 15-21.

Responsorial Psalm
"Sing to the Lord all the earth". Choose a song that you all know. *Say* a verse and then *sing* the same verse. Which version sounds the happier?
— "Tell his wonders among all the people". Think of three things that are wonderful because they are so small.
— "Bring an offering and enter his courts". What part of the Mass does this remind you of? After the priest has offered the bread and wine, he says this prayer quietly:

> Lord God, we ask you to receive us
> and be pleased with the sacrifice we offer you
> with humble and contrite hearts.

Gospel Reading

If you have young children in your family, they may like to "rub" a coin by placing it under a piece of paper and going over it with a pencil or crayon.

— Is this money any good for buying things in another country? Why not?

— Read the passage in which the enemies of Jesus tried to trap him. If he said: "You mustn't pay your taxes to Caesar", how would he have been in trouble?
If he said: "You must pay your taxes to Caesar", he would have become very unpopular with the people who hated the Roman rule. He didn't want to get involved in a political discussion. How did Jesus get out of the trap?

Prayer together

> We are part of creation, made by God. Let us thank him for all he has given us.
> He has given each one of us special gifts to use in his service. Let us think for a moment of the gifts and talents he has given us.
> Lord God, give us strength and joy in serving you as followers of Christ.

30th Sunday of the Year   *Cycle A*

THE COMMANDMENT OF LOVE

Prepare your Bible

Old Testament: Exodus, ch. 22, vv, 20-26.
New Testament: St Matthew, ch. 22, vv. 34-40.

Opening prayer

> Almighty and ever-living God,
> strengthen our faith, hope and love.
> May we do with loving hearts
> what you ask of us
> and come to share the life you promise.

First Reading

God gave Moses the Ten Commandments so that the Children of Israel should have some guidance how to live in God's way. The Israelites gradually built up other laws as they became necessary.

— How did God ask that one should behave towards:—
       strangers,
       widows and orphans,
       those who borrow money,
       those who leave their cloak as a pledge?

Gospel Reading

The Pharisees and Sadducees were Jewish sects who usually disagreed with one another. In this case, their hatred for Jesus brought them together.

— Read the text.
— Do you agree that we can only love people that we know? And that the more we love someone, the more we want to know them?
— Are we more ready to help those we know and love than strangers? Why is this?
— Who did Jesus mean by "your neighbour?" Is this easy?
— If we fail, and we may fail very often, what can we do?

Prayer

Say slowly and thoughtfully the opening prayer.

31st Sunday of the Year   *Cycle A*

AT YOUR SERVICE

Things you need

A match box. A piece of tape or ribbon long enough to tie round someone's head to hold the match box in place on the forehead. Write on a piece of paper: "Hear O Israel, the Lord your God is one God". Fold it and put it inside the match box.

Prepare your Bible

Old Testament: Malachi, ch. 1, v. 14 — ch. 2, vv. 2, 8-10.
New Testament: 1 Thessalonians, ch. 2, vv. 7-9, 13;
St Matthew, ch. 23, vv. 1-12.

First Reading

Malachi was a prophet who lived about 500 years before Christ. Read the warnings he is giving to the priests of the time. They have ceased to give God due honour and they have led their people astray.

Second Reading

What a contrast! How does St Paul feel about the new Christians in Thessalonica?

— Besides actually preaching the Good News to the people, what did Paul and his friends obviously do as well? v. 9.
— St Paul says that the message "is still a living power among you who believe it".

This is the Prayer after Communion:

Lord,
you give us new hope in this eucharist.
May the power of your love
continue its saving work among us
and bring us to the joy you promise.

Gospel Reading

In this talk, Jesus speaks very harshly about the scribes and the Pharisees much as Malachi did many years before.

Look at the match box you have prepared to show what a phylactery was like. This is the little box that was fastened round the head. The message inside from the Torah (the Jewish Law) was a constant reminder of God.

— Why do we dislike people who show-off?
— Do you think people sometimes show-off by what they wear? by what they say? by what they do?
— Do you think they are happy and at peace when they act in this way?
— vv. 11, 12. Sometimes the Pope calls himself 'the servant of the servants of God'. What does this mean?
— If you have been to the Mass of the Last Supper on Maundy Thursday, you will have seen a great symbol of the service your bishop or your parish priest wish to give to their people. What is this action?

79

BE PREPARED

Prepare your Bible

Old Testament: Wisdom, ch. 6, vv. 12-16.
New Testament: St Matthew, ch. 25, vv. 1-13.

First Reading

(St Paul told the Corinthians that "Christ is the power and wisdom of God".) Wisdom was greatly desired by the people of the Old Testament. Would you say that wise people are always good people? Can you think of some phrases using the word "wisdom?"

Read this passage again substituting "the love of Jesus" for the word "wisdom". Talk about each phrase and see how true it is.

Gospel Reading

You remember that a parable is a story with a hidden meaning. We are very nearly at the end of the Church's year and then Advent will begin. The Alleluia verse this Sunday introduces the message of this Gospel.

> Alleluia, Alleluia!
> Stay awake and stand ready,
> because you do not know the hour
> when the Son of Man is coming.
> Alleluia!

Read the Gospel. Can you make up a modern parable with the same meaning? Here are some hints: — Have you enough petrol in the car? Have you enough ink in your pen? Have you kept your washing up to date? Have you kept a 5p piece for the gas meter?

Behind the parable that Jesus told was a very serious meaning. We don't know when God our Father will call us to go home to him. We pray that we will be ready with a free and loving heart to go to join him in heaven when he calls us (comes to fetch us).

LIVING FOR GOD

Prepare your Bible

Old Testament: Proverbs, ch. 31, vv. 10-13, 19-20, 30-31;
          Psalm 127 (128), Happy are those . . . .
New Testament: St Matthew, ch. 25, vv. 14-30.

Introduction

We can think of Christ as head of the family, the Church, and so the readings show how various members of the family bring their love and service.

First Reading

First we have a picture of the wife in a family. Read the passage together and then think of a modern example for each of these verses:

— She is always busy with wool and flax,
— She sets her hands to the distaff,
  her fingers grasp the spindle.

Would you say that the other verses are as true today as they were when they were written, many years before Christ?

Responsorial Psalm

Your wife like a fruitful vine, in the heart of your house;
your children like shoots of the olive, around your table.

Why do you think the psalmist chose these comparisons?

Gospel Reading

Before you read this passage, work out the sums of money involved so that you can read the English equivalent. A talent is approximately £300.

— What did each of the three servants do with the money they had been put in charge of?
— Why did the third man make no attempt to use it for his master?

F

The hidden meaning

If we take the other meaning of the word "talent", let us think of the talents God has given each of us to use in his service.

Prayer

Father, sometimes we have wasted the talents you give us: instead of our best, the work we offered was often performed hastily and half-heartedly. — Lord, have mercy.

When tasks proved difficult, we gave up too easily and failed to persevere. — Christ, have mercy.

Golden opportunities to develop our skills or deepen our knowledge we threw away, unused. — Lord, have mercy.

Father, we rejoice in your forgiveness and we dedicate ourselves again to your service with the help of Christ Our Lord. Amen.

Last Sunday of the Year

CHRIST THE KING

Things you need

Ask each member of the family to bring something which seems to represent the main part of their life at present — e.g., if you are at school, a school book or football; mother may bring a Hoover or washing-up liquid; father may bring car keys or computer paper or hammer; grandad may bring a spade or packet of seeds!

Make a crown for each person from a strip of paper. Staple or glue the ends together. Decorate it with crayons.

Preface of the Mass

Father, all-powerful and ever-living God,
we do well always and everywhere to give you thanks.

You anointed Jesus Christ, your only Son, with the oil of gladness,
as the eternal priest and universal king.

As priest he offered his life on the altar of the cross
and redeemed the human race
by this one perfect sacrifice of peace.

As king he claims dominion over all creation,
that he may present to you, his almighty Father,
an eternal and universal kingdom:
a kingdom of truth and life,
a kingdom of holiness and grace,
a kingdom of justice, love, and peace.

— What do we specially want to thank God for, TODAY?

— Jesus is king of all the world and of 'the little world that is me'.

Put the things you have brought in the middle of the table or on the floor. Look at each one in turn and help each other to see how our lives can show the signs of Christ's kingdom:

truth	life	
holiness		grace (God's life in me)
justice	love	peace

Prayer

Place your crown on the 'symbol' of your life. Say, as you do so, 'Lord Jesus Christ, be king of my life'.

Something to do

Use your crowns as decoration for your meal table or your room for tomorrow, Sunday.

— 'Jesus Christ . . . . the Ruler of the kings of the earth . . . . he has loved us . . . . and made us a line of kings . . . .'

Cycle B

WAITING

Things you need

An Advent wreath (see page 14). Some withered leaves. An alarm clock, tin of coffee or packet of tea.

Prepare your Bible

Old Testament: Isaiah, ch. 63, vv. 16, 17, ch. 64, vv. 1, 3-8.
New Testament: 1 Corinthians, ch. 1, vv. 3-9;
St Mark, ch. 13, vv. 33-37.

To start you talking

Have you ever had visitors who arrived before you were ready for them? What happened in your home when they rang or knocked at the door? Where is the best 'lookout' post in your house to see the visitors coming?

First Reading

Isaiah was putting into words the great longing of the Jewish people for God to make himself known to them. They were waiting for the Messiah to come to save them.

v. 6   Why do leaves wither on the tree? What do you think had happened to the Jews for Isaiah to choose this picture to describe them?

v. 8   Have you worked or seen anyone work with clay? How does it feel to mould the clay to any shape you like? Why does Isaiah choose this picture? If God is the potter, how beautiful his work must be! We are the work of his hands. 'God made me'.

Second Reading

Think of the teachers and priests who have specially helped you. Say a 'Glory be to the Father' in thanksgiving for them all.

v. 8   He will keep you steady and without blame until the last day, the day of Our Lord Jesus Christ. Why?

Gospel Reading

Light the first candle of your Advent wreath. Stand up and listen to the Gospel — standing is a position of readiness. It's easier to stay awake if you are standing! Sit down to talk and pray.

Why have we brought an alarm clock and tea or coffee?

How can we keep 'awake' for Jesus to speak to us and come to dwell in us?

Advent is the time when we try to prepare for the Coming of Christ — a) At our Christmas Communion and celebration.
b) At his Second Coming.

Which do you think Jesus was referring to when he told this story?

Prayer

May God make us steadfast in faith, joyful in hope and untiring in love.

2nd Sunday of Advent   *Cycle B*

PREPARING

Things you need

Your Advent wreath. A sandal.

Prepare your Bible

Old Testament: Isaiah, ch. 40, vv. 1-5, 9-11.
New Testament: St Mark, ch. 1, vv. 1-8.

Opening prayer

God of power and mercy,
open our hearts in welcome.
Remove the things that hinder us from receiving Christ with joy.

— What things do we mean? Perhaps not noticing people who need our help; perhaps not saying 'sorry' quickly when we have hurt someone; perhaps not quietening our hearts when we pray . . . .
— You could say the prayer again.

First Reading

This prayer is echoed in the message from Isaiah.

— vv. 1, 2. 'God of mercy'. God sends words of comfort to his people. Why?

— vv. 3, 4, 5. 'Open our hearts'. What picture is painted to show how we are to make God's entry into our hearts an easy one?

— v. 9. 'Joy'. What words are used to show that the message 'Here is our God' is a joyful one?

— vv. 10, 11. 'God of power'. Yes, our God is triumphant but he is loving and he cares for his people. How does Isaiah make us understand this?

Gospel Reading

Light two candles on your Advent wreath and then read the Gospel.

— How does St Mark show that John the Baptist was heralding the Messiah for whom all the Jews were waiting?

— How did John prepare himself for his great work of introducing Jesus?

— What did he ask of the people who came to be baptised?

— How does this link up with our prayer?

— How did John show that he knew how much greater was the Messiah he was heralding than he himself?

Something to do

Make a plan to celebrate the Sacrament of Reconciliation before Christmas. This meeting with Jesus in Confession is the best way to 'remove the things that hinder us from receiving Christ with joy'. This sacrament is sometimes called a "Second Baptism". Why?

Prayer

Say the opening prayer quietly and thoughtfully.

REJOICING

Things you need

Your Advent wreath. Christmas cards that you have already received, especially those showing candles or other lights.

Prepare your Bible

Old Testament: Isaiah, ch. 61, vv. 1, 2, 10, 11.
New Testament: 1 Thessalonians, ch. 5, v. 16.
St John, ch. 1, vv. 6-8, 19-28.

First Reading

We look upon this text as referring to Jesus. Who sent Jesus on his mission?

Advent is the time when we prepare to celebrate Christ's *coming.* Christ comes to work through us and in us: so how can we

— give good news to the poor? People in any great *need* are poor: the homeless, the lonely, those with a great need to be forgiven, or understood, or supported in their daily life.

— bind up hearts that are broken? Is there anyone we ought to write to this Christmas because they are sad?

— proclaim liberty to captives? Fear can take us captive. Is there anyone who is scared of us because of our teasing or impatience? What can we do?

Second Reading

St Paul tells us to be happy at all times. This Advent is a time to be happy, to pray a little more, to thank God for his goodness. Could we find a way in our family to do these three things as a preparation for Christmas?

Gospel Reading

Light three candles on your wreath. Once more we have a quotation from Isaiah as John's answer to the people who were puzzled by him. At first the Jews thought that John was the Messiah. You will notice that this Sunday and last Sunday the Gospel is telling us about events when Jesus was grown-up. How do we know that John was aware that Jesus was waiting for the right moment to show himself?

A Prayer together

Look at your Christmas cards and pray for the senders. Perhaps you could take it in turn to read the names; e.g., This is from Auntie Eileen: Lord God, fill Auntie Eileen with joy this Christmas.

4th Sunday of Advent   *Cycle B*

PROMISING

Things you need

Your Advent wreath. Christmas Cards you have received during the week. Choose your favourite card of Our Lady.

Prepare your Bible

Old Testament: 2 Samuel, ch. 7, vv. 1-5, 8-11, 16.
New Testament: St Luke, ch. 1, vv. 26-38.

First Reading

The Israelites believed that God's presence was specially with them in the Ark of the Covenant. The Ark of the Covenant was a big rectangular box or chest made of very precious wood and covered with gold. In it was contained a copy of the Law of God — the contract made between God and his people. The Ark was kept in a special tent and was considered to be the greatest sign or symbol of God's presence. When the people went on their long journey to Palestine God dwelt with them and led them in the march. Why did David feel it was unsuitable for the Ark to be in a tent? What does a cedar tree look like? Do you know anything made of cedar wood?

God would not let King David build this house. He had something much greater in his mind. "Your House and your sovereignty will always stand secure . . ." What does this refer to?

We often sing a carol referring to Royal David's city. What city is this? We also sing, "To you in David's town this day is born . . ." Can you finish the line? What is the connection with this reading?

Gospel Reading

God had prepared his chosen people for years; at last the time was ripe for the Redeemer to come. God chose an Israelite girl, Mary, to be the Ark of the Covenant in a very special way. How? Mary was one of us, an ordinary human being. She shows us the way to respond to God's call — in complete trust. What was the result of her "Yes"?

Prayer together

You could pray with your Christmas cards as you did last week. You could take as the refrain some words from the Opening Prayer of the Mass. "Lord, fill our hearts with your love".

Sunday in the Octave of Christmas — see page 18

2nd Sunday after Christmas — see page 19

Sunday after the Epiphany — see page 20

1st Sunday of Lent   *Cycle B*

SIDE BY SIDE WITH JESUS

Things you need

Write the word COVENANT on a card and in smaller letters write "pledge, promise, agreement, contract, pact". Think of examples of the use of these words, e.g. buying a house, being enrolled as a Scout or Guide, getting married, etc.

Prepare your Bible

Old Testament: Genesis, ch. 9, vv. 8-15.

New Testament: 1 Peter, ch. 3, vv. 18-22;
St Mark, ch. 1, vv. 12-15.

First Reading

Throughout the Old Testament we are told of the many, many times God made a covenant with his people. God never broke his promise to them though they were often unfaithful to their side of the bargain.

— What was the promise God made to Noah? What sign did God choose to reassure his people that he would keep his promise? Why was this a good sign to choose for this particular promise?

Response to the Psalm

"Your ways, Lord, are faithfulness and love
for those who keep your covenant".

Think of some ways in which we keep our side of the covenant with God by our prayer, the way we live, our attitude to other people.

Second Reading

Notice how St Peter links up the story of Noah with our baptism. In the waters of the flood, the beauty and order of creation was almost destroyed. It was as if evil had triumphed. By God's power, from these very same waters, one family was rescued and goodness, beauty and love were to spread over the world again. St Peter explains that when we are baptised, it is with Jesus and by his power that we will prevent evil overcoming our life and our world. Evil could  drown us but it will not do so, if we remain with Jesus. What word is used to show that baptism is a covenant between God and ourselves?

This is the greatest covenant — God is our Father, we are his children. He gives us his very life at baptism, and we are given this gift, thanks to the death and resurrection of Jesus Christ.

Gospel Reading

Lent has begun for us this year. For these forty days especially we will try to become more like Jesus — we want to be led by the Holy Spirit.

We may be tempted by Satan, we may meet "wild beasts" of hate and anger, but we, baptised Christians, are never alone in difficulties.

And at the end of Lent, we must be more ready than ever before to say, "Believe the Good News. Jesus is alive".

Prayer
> Father,
> through our observance of Lent,
> help us to understand the meaning
> of your Son's death and resurrection,
> and teach us to reflect it in our lives.

2nd Sunday of Lent   *Cycle B*

THE GREAT GIFT

Things you need
A crucifix as a reminder that Lent is leading us to Good Friday.

Prepare your Bible
Old Testament: Genesis, ch. 22, vv. 1-2, 9-13, 15-18.
New Testament: Romans, ch. 8, vv. 31-34;
St Mark, ch. 9, vv. 2-10.

First Reading
This seems a very terrible story — read it and then discuss how Abraham must have felt and how the little son must have felt when he realised what his father was going to do. Abraham was about to make a terrible mistake because he was influenced by his pagan neighbours. (Abraham was ready to give to God the best he had.) However, his heart was in the right place and God was able to get through to his conscience and say, "No! No human sacrifice".

Second Reading
In this reading, St Paul reminds us that 'God did not spare his own Son, but gave him up to benefit us all'.

— What did Jesus suffer? (not just physically).

— What did this mean to his Mother?

After his death came the resurrection — NEW LIFE — and this was not only for him but *for all of us.*

Gospel Reading — (2nd Sunday of Lent, Cycle A or C)

If you want to discuss this, turn to page 23 or 159, but there is a special Preface for this Sunday you might like to read.

Father, all-powerful and ever-living God,
we do well always and everywhere to give you thanks
through Jesus Christ our Lord.

On your holy mountain he revealed himself in glory
in the presence of his disciples.
He had already prepared them for his approaching death.
He wanted to teach them through the Law and the Prophets
that the promised Christ had first to suffer
and so come to the glory of his resurrection.

In unending joy we echo on earth
the song of the angels in heaven
as they praise your glory for ever: Holy, holy . . . .

— Which disciples were with Jesus on the mountain?

— Jesus had prepared them for his death, but had they fully understood?

— Which prophets did they see? Which of these two prophets had given the Law to the Chosen People?

— Would the disciples have understood what "rising from the dead" could mean?

LIVING IN GOD'S WAY

Things you need
Your crucifix where everyone can see it while you work.

Prepare your Bible
Old Testament: Exodus, ch. 20, vv. 1-3, 7-8, 12-17.
New Testament: St John, ch. 2, vv. 15-25.

First Reading
When the children of Israel were ready for some sort of guidelines in order to live as God's people, these Laws were given to them to help them to live together in peace and happiness.

Here are some questions to discuss:

— Do people sometimes make gods of other things in their lives instead of worshipping God?
— You must not make any images to *worship.* Why do we have statues in our churches and in our schools or homes?
— How can we be tempted to use God's name in a wrong way?
— How can we keep Sunday holy?
— Do not despise your father and mother. Does this ever happen?
— Is killing ever justified?
— You must not commit adultery. Is this Law still needed?
— Is it possible to steal time? — from an employer, for instance?
— False witness. What does this mean?
— Is there a temptation today to covet our neighbour's new car or record player or colour TV, etc. . . .?

Prayer
Father,
you have taught us to overcome our sins
by prayer, fasting and works of mercy.
When we are discouraged by our weakness,
give us confidence in your love.

96

Gospel Reading

In the time of Jesus, the Jews still held to their practice of offering God the sacrifice of animals in the Temple at Jerusalem. This seemed the perfect, complete gift of life where blood was spilt and the flesh was burned for God's sake so that nothing was left. Jesus had come to show that this was only a step towards real sacrifice for God which is a life spent in his loving service. Jesus himself was to give his life on the cross.

To buy an animal or bird for sacrifice, it was necessary to have Temple-money, and the money changers were often swindlers. But Jesus wanted God his Father to be worshipped in a prayerful, loving, reverent way — not amongst a mixture of noise and dishonesty.

— In your own church, what things or actions help you to realise the presence of God and encourage you to be reverent? Can you remember any time specially when you felt that God was being worshipped and loved by you and the people you were with?

4th Sunday of Lent   *Cycle B*
(The readings of Cycle A may be used, p. 26)

CHRIST OUR MODEL

Things you need

Your crucifix and a lighted candle to focus your attention.

Prepare your Bible

Old Testament: 2 Chronicles, ch. 36, vv. 14-16, 19-23.
New Testament: Ephesians, ch. 2, vv. 4-10;
            St John, ch. 3, vv. 14-21.

First Reading

On the first Sunday of Lent this year, we spoke about the COVENANT made between God and man. Today we read of all the efforts God made to bring his people back to him when they refused his friendship and disobeyed the Laws he had given for their happiness.

— What happened to the Temple?

G

— What happened to Jerusalem?
— What happened to God's own people?
— Why did these tragedies, so opposed to God's love, come about?
— Then it was a foreign king who, in the end, recreated the city and the Temple. Who did he invite to help him?

Second Reading

During Lent, we think about putting our life a little more in order. Sometimes we think that by forcing ourselves to keep our Lent resolutions, we are making ourselves better people. Perhaps we are! But in this reading St Paul tells us that everything is a gift from God, especially our friendship with him. Read how St Paul expresses it.

Just think of it — "We are God's work of art, created in Jesus Christ to live the good life as from the beginning he meant us to live it". — Let us thank God for making us.

Gospel Reading

Read this passage and then look carefully at verse 21.
— Can you think of any incident when people have followed the light of their conscience against public opinion?
— Is it always possible to do this?
— What risks may be involved?

Prayer after Communion

Father,
you enlighten all who come into the world.
Fill our hearts with the light of your gospel,
that our thoughts may please you,
and our love be sincere.
We ask this through Christ our Lord. Amen.

5th Sunday of Lent   *Cycle B*

DYING TO OURSELVES

Things you need

Your crucifix. Some grain or rice or a packet of seed.

Prepare your Bible

Old Testament: Jeremiah, ch. 31, vv. 31-34.
New Testament: St John, ch. 12, vv. 20-33.

First Reading

Once again we meet the word COVENANT. It shows that God loves us so much that he continues to give opportunities to his people to come back to him. In this reading God is looking far forward to the time when, Jeremiah says, "I will be their God and they will be my people".

— Which phrase makes you think of a gardener? What is the seed and where is the soil? (v. 33)

Gospel Reading

The Liturgy at this time of the year is leading us gradually to approach the Passion of Jesus. People, like the Greeks in the incident, who want to know Jesus, must be prepared for the pattern of death and resurrection in their own lives.

— If your grain or rice or seed remains in its packet, will it germinate and grow? Of course not. It must be put in the dark, dirty soil where it risks being forgotten. Only like this will it sprout and become a plant.
— How does this apply to the life of a Christian?
— Why did this description of the seed illustrate what was going to happen to Jesus?
— Find words of Jesus in this Gospel which show that he was dreading what lay ahead of him.
— Find the words that assure us that by his death, Jesus conquered, for ever, the power of evil.
— What words show that Jesus was absolutely sure of his mission in the world and of the way to carry it out?

Opening Prayer of the Mass

We may be tested by illness or misfortune or sorrow. We may be troubled now as we pray together. We may have friends who are in distress. Let us pray for courage to follow Christ:

Father,
help us to be more like Christ your Son,
who loved the world and died for our salvation.
Inspire us by his love,
guide us by his example,
who lives and reigns with you and the Holy Spirit,
one God, for ever and ever. Amen.

Passion Sunday — see page 29

Easter Sunday — see page 30

2nd Sunday of Easter   *Cycle B*

UNITED IN FAITH

Things you need

Your Easter candle with flowers. The word "PEACE" written on a card and decorated.

Prepare your Bible

New Testament: Acts, ch. 4, vv. 32-35;
St John, ch. 20, vv. 19-31.

First Reading

Our family is the Church in miniature. What things do we share with each other — rooms, TV, clothes, writing materials, talents, joy, sympathy . . .? What kind of things do we share with friends outside the family?

How does our parish family make sure that "none of its members is ever in want"?

AND ALL THIS BECAUSE JESUS IS ALIVE.

Gospel Reading

How would you describe the change of atmosphere in the room when 'Jesus came and stood among the disciples'? What was his greeting to them?

Some Christians these days greet each other in the same way or they use a Jewish greeting, 'Shalom'. Do you know the song which begins with this word?

What sacrament did Jesus put into the power of his priests? 'Thomas was not with them'. Probably in his misery he had gone off by himself. But Jesus waited for him to be with his friends before giving him a chance to make his act of faith. We, too, need to come to Christ with our friends and to accept the companionship and support of each other. We can say the words of Thomas as we look up at the moment of the consecration of the Mass.

'This is my Body . . . .'   'My Lord and my God'
'This is my Blood . . . .'   'My Lord and my God'

And Jesus says to each of us, 'Happy are those who have not seen and yet believe'.

Prayer together

> God of mercy,
> you wash away our sins in water,
> you give us new birth in the Spirit,
> and redeem us in the blood of Christ.
> As we celebrate Christ's resurrection
> increase our awareness of these blessings,
> and renew your gift of life within us.

3rd Sunday of Easter   *Cycle B*

FROM ALARM AND FRIGHT
TO PEACE AND JOY

Things you need

Your Easter candle and flowers. Write these words in a higgledy-piggledy way on a page — alarm, fright, agitated, doubts, peace, joy.

Prepare your Bible

New Testament: Acts, ch. 3, vv. 13-15, 17-19;
St Luke, ch. 24, vv. 35-48.

First Reading

This speech of Peter took place after Pentecost, when he had been strengthened and enlightened by the Holy Spirit.

— Do you think Peter took any risks in speaking in such an outspoken way to the people?

— Peter refers to Jesus in five different ways. Can you find them?

— Who is the murderer Peter refers to?

— In spite of his accusations, Peter makes excuses for the people and he tells them the way they can come back to God. What does he tell them?

Gospel Reading

How difficult it was for the disciples to believe that Jesus really was alive!

— How did Jesus prove to them that he was not a ghost?

— What is a witness?

— How was Jesus making sure that his disciples would be reliable and convinced witnesses?

Prayer together

St Luke tells us that Jesus 'opened their minds to understand the scriptures'.

Let us ask Our Lord to open our minds, *(pause)*

to calm our fears, *(pause)*

to free us from being too occupied with ourselves. *(pause)*

Lord Jesus, explain the scriptures to us.
Make our hearts burn within us as you talk to us.
Help us to be your witnesses.
Amen.

4th Sunday of Easter   **Cycle B**

GOOD SHEPHERD SUNDAY

Things you need

Your Easter candle. A picture of sheep or a shepherd. (Young children may have farmyard sheep or a cuddly toy.)

Prepare your Bible

New Testament: Acts, ch. 4, vv. 8-12;
St John, ch.. 10, vv. 11-18.

First Reading

(The person leading today's study should be prepared to tell the story found in Acts, ch. 3, vv. 1-10.)

Here is Peter, 'filled with the Holy Spirit', speaking out bravely and convincingly once again. To whom is he speaking? What attitude does he sense in his hearers?

How wonderful Jesus is! He went through death to life. He was rejected by those who thought they represented God's authority.

Peter speaks of Jesus, not only as *a* stone in a building, but as *the key-stone*. Do you know what this means? Why is it a good description of Jesus?

The response to the Responsorial Psalm on Sunday is: "The stone which the builders rejected has become the cornerstone". Is the cornerstone the same as a key-stone?

Gospel Reading

We read in the Gospel of the description that Jesus chose for himself — a real, loving, hardworking, caring person.

— Why does a hired man desert the sheep when danger looms up?

— Jesus said: "I lay down my life for my sheep".
"I lay down my life in order to take it up again".

What do we understand Jesus to mean? Would the disciples have understood what Jesus meant?

— Jesus said: 'There are other sheep I have that are not of this fold, and these I have to lead as well . . . There will be only one flock and one shepherd'.

What do you think Jesus meant by this? Is it applicable to us today? Think of some ways in which Christians are trying to make this possible.

Prayer

> Almighty and ever-living God,
> give us new strength
> from the courage of Christ our Shepherd,
> and lead us to join the saints in heaven.

5th Sunday of Easter   **Cycle B**

ONE WITH CHRIST

Things you need

Your Easter candle. A picture of a vine or grapes. A pair of secateurs. Map of Palestine in the time of Christ.

Prepare your Bible

New Testament: Acts, ch. 9, vv. 26-31;
                         1 John, ch. 3, vv. 18-24;
                         St John, ch. 15, vv. 1-8.

First Reading

The leader should make sure he can recount the conversion of Saul (see Acts, ch. 9).

Read the passage slowly to the family, giving time for the place to be found on your map.

Why were people, even the disciples, suspicious of Saul? Who was Saul's great support?

It is sometimes difficult to be accepted when one has had a bad name. Think of people released from prison. Do they find it easy to obtain work?

Second Reading

See how John in his letter gives us courage to turn over a new leaf, knowing that God sees into our hearts and loves us. "Whatever we ask of God, we shall receive".

Gospel Reading

— Read the whole passage and then look at verse 5. Jesus says: "I am the vine. You are the branches". He doesn't say he is the trunk and we are the branches. What difference does that make?

— "A branch that does bear fruit he prunes". What other trees and bushes need pruning? Would you know how to prune a tree? Used skilfully, your secateurs can help to bring new life to a tree, but used in an unskilled or unloving hand what might happen?

— St Paul tells us that the fruits of the Spirit are love, joy, peace, patience, kindness, goodness, trustfulness, gentleness and self-control. This is why God prunes us in various ways.

In verse 4, Jesus tells us that unless we remain in him, we cannot bear fruit. How can we "remain in him?"

Final blessing

Lord,
help your people to seek you with all their hearts
and to deserve what you promise.
Grant this through Christ our Lord. Amen.
And may the blessing of almighty God,
the Father, and the Son, and the Holy Spirit,
come upon us and remain with us for ever. Amen.

6th Sunday of Easter   **Cycle B**

SMILE, GOD LOVES YOU

Things you need
Your Easter candle. Make a large Smiley picture.

Prepare your Bible

New Testament: Acts, ch. 10, vv. 25-26, 34-35, 44-48;
                1 John, ch. 4, vv. 7-10;
                St John, ch. 15, vv. 9-17.

First Reading

Cornelius was a Roman centurion who respected and was generous to the Jews. God introduced him to Peter through a dream (see the beginning of the chapter). Also through a dream God made Peter understand that *all men* were to hear the Good News. How did Peter explain this to Cornelius when they met?

— Notice how the Holy Spirit came upon these Jews before they were baptised with water.

Second Reading

St John is well-known for his insistence on the importance of love. How many times does he speak of love in these few verses?

Gospel Reading

This continues last week's Gospel. Jesus is trying to help us to understand how deep is his love for us.

— Twice in this passage Jesus says: "If . . .". Find out what he says.
— What is the difference between a servant and a friend?
— The word Gospel means G . . . N . . . so presumably it brings happiness. A much stronger word for happiness is used in this passage. What is it?

What hymns or songs containing this word can you think of?

Prayer

    Ever-living God,
    help us to celebrate our joy
    in the resurrection of the Lord
    and to express in our lives
    the love we celebrate.

CONSECRATED IN TRUTH

Things you need
Your Easter candle.

Prepare your Bible
New Testament: Acts, ch. 1, vv. 15-17, 20-26;
                        St John, ch. 17, vv. 11-19.

First Reading
— What were the qualifications needed for the man who was to replace Judas Iscariot?
— Who was nominated?
— Read the apostles' prayer for guidance.
— How was Matthias chosen?

Gospel Reading
This is part of the prayer of Jesus for his disciples — not just for the ones gathered round the table at the Last Supper, but for all of us, centuries later.
— "Keep those you have given me true to your name". — In the Creed we say, "We believe . . .". This is the truth to which we hold.
— "I am not asking you to remove them from the world, but to protect them from the evil one". In the "Our Father" we ask for this. Which phrase?
— "As you have sent me into the world, I have sent them into the world". Christ sends us as Christians into our schools, factories, offices, fields. How can we be faithful witnesses to God's love in the places where we work and play?

Prayer
Let us pray that we may recognise the presence of Christ in our midst. (Pause for recollection.)

Father,
help us to keep in mind that Christ our Saviour
lives with you in glory
and promised to remain with us until the end of time.

Pentecost — see page 39

Trinity Sunday — see page 40

2nd Sunday of the Year   *Cycle B*

"COME"

Things you need

A mat or folded blanket in the corner of the room. A lamp or candle. Christian names of each member of your family written on separate pieces of paper.

Prepare your Bible

Old Testament: 1 Samuel, ch. 3, vv. 3-10, 19.
New Testament: St John, ch. 1, vv. 35-42.

To talk about

Find out why your names were chosen for you. Were you named after a relative? Is yours the name of a favourite saint? Did your parents like the sound of your name? Was the name decided before you were born? If you have a nickname, who uses it and when?

First Reading

Ask one member of your family to be Samuel (lying on the mat or blanket) so that you can act the story as it is read. Light the candle or lamp.

— You remember how Mary and Joseph redeemed Jesus on the day of his presentation in the Temple. In the time of Samuel, every first born son had to be presented in the Temple and left there to serve God. This was to keep alive the memory of God's goodness to the Israelites when the angel of death "passed over" their homes but killed all the first born in the Egyptians' homes.

Gospel Reading

Read the account of the call of the first disciples as John tells it. These men were already followers of John the Baptist and they had to leave him in order to become followers of Jesus.

— What did John the Baptist call Jesus when he pointed him out to his own disciples? When do *we* hear the same phrase?

— Andrew took his brother meet Jesus the next day.

Jesus gave Peter a new name to show that a change was taking place in his life.

When we are given our names at Baptism, what change takes place in our lives?

If you took a special name at your Confirmation, this was to mark yet another change, a special step forward in your friendship with Jesus Christ.

Prayer

The response to the psalm is:

"Here I am Lord! I come to do your will!" and Samuel's reply to God was, "Speak Lord, your servant is listening".

Say the names of each member of your family in turn. Let them reply out loud or in their hearts with one of these responses.

3rd Sunday of the Year   **Cycle B**

ON A MISSION

Things you need

Piece of hessian or an old sack. Picture of fishermen or of a fishing boat from a book or magazine.

Prepare your Bible

Old Testament: Jonah, ch. 3, vv. 1-5, 10.
New Testament: St Mark, ch. 1, vv. 14-20.

First Reading

The first time God asked Jonah to be his messenger, Jonah decided to run away from God. He took a ship at Joppa and we all know what happened! (Jonah, ch. 1 and 2.) Then God asked Jonah again to be his messenger. What was the message?

Why do you think Jonah hadn't wanted to go the first time? He must have preached well because the people listened to his unpleasant message and repented — changed their ways and believed in God. What did they do to show they were sorry for the way they had been living?

Gospel Reading

— Why was John the Baptist in prison? (The leader this week could look up St Matthew, ch. 14, vv. 1-5 in advance).
— Do you think it would have been better for John to hold his tongue about Herod's behaviour in order to stay out of prison and help his cousin Jesus?
— You notice that St Mark's account of the call of the first disciples is slightly different from the way St John told us last week.

Why did Jesus say, "I will make you fishers of men"?

Find some comparisons between fishing and bringing people to know Jesus.

E.g. who are the fish?

where do you throw out your nets?

what is the purpose of bait?

can you fish all day and all night?

Prayer

Because we are baptised, we have a mission to show Christ to the people we meet by the way we live. Sometimes we can be like Jonah and try to run away from what God is asking us to do for him. Let us pray that we will be more like Andrew, Peter, John and James in our following of Jesus.

All-powerful and ever-living God,
direct your love that is within us,
so that our efforts in the name of your Son
may bring mankind to unity and peace.

110

SPEAKING FOR GOD

Things you need

Write out the opening prayer of the Mass like this:

"Lord our God,

help us/them to love you with all our/their hearts
and to love all men as you love them".

Make a copy for each member of your family.

Prepare your Bible

Old Testament: Deuteronomy, ch. 18, vv. 15-20.
New Testament: St Mark, ch. 1, vv. 21-28.

First Reading

This passage comes from a very long set of instructions which Moses was giving to the Chosen People, the Israelites on their way to the Promised Land. Moses knew that he himself was not to be allowed by God to enter this Land. He believed that God would always take care of his people by sending other leaders to encourage them and to keep them in touch with God.

— "I will raise up a prophet for them from their own brothers". Priests come from families like our own. They try to live close to God and to pass on to us the Good News of the love of God. Remind each other of the priests you know and say together the prayer your leader has copied out for each of you. Let us ask God to call many boys to be priests and to give them the courage to say like the psalmist: "Lord, make me know your ways".

Gospel Reading

Jesus was a Jew and he would go to the synagogue to worship every Sabbath day. Perhaps the "rulers" of the synagogue had heard about him and had invited him to preach.

— Why was the teaching of Jesus unlike the scribes?
— What was this authority that they felt?
— The sick man recognised Jesus. How did Jesus heal him?

— Can you think of an example of someone teaching you when:
   a) they were just using a book to give you facts; and
   b) they knew from experience what they were talking about.

Prayer

If we are to be followers of Jesus and bring others to know him, we must speak from experience. Let us say the opening prayer of the Mass together — first for ourselves, "Help us"; and then for the people we shall meet during this week, "Help them".

5th Sunday of the Year   *Cycle B*

WE NEED TO PRAY

Things you need
A picture of a sunset and of a lonely countryside.

Prepare your Bible
Old Testament: Job, ch. 7, vv. 1-4, 6-7.
New Testament: St Mark, ch. 1, vv. 29-39.

First Reading
The book of Job is made up of the Prologue and Epilogue of an old folktale written in prose.

Our reading today is part of the beautiful poem which comes between them. The story is of a rich man Job and his family who are struck by terrible disasters until at the end all is well again.
— Read the passage. What mood is Job in?
— How does he describe his disillusionment with life?
— Can you think of any people today who might be feeling some of these things? Could we pray for them?

"Father, watch over your family and keep them safe in your care, for all our hope is in you".

Read Job's final answer to God in ch. 42, vv. 1-6.

Gospel Reading

Read the passage and see if you think of any of the people mentioned that could have been feeling like Job before Jesus came to them.

— How do we know that Peter was married?
— Why did the people wait till after sunset to bring their sick friends and relations to Jesus? (v. 29 gives the clue.)
— What does v. 35 tell us about Jesus and his prayer?
— It is good to pray together at Mass, to pray in the family but we also need to pray alone. Talk a little about your favourite place for prayer. Perhaps you can remember an occasion on holiday, at camp, in the snow, up a tree when you were alone and glad to be with God. If you live near enough to a church, perhaps you can pay a quiet visit to the Blessed Sacrament sometimes. As an old man once said when asked what he did when he went into church: "I looks at him and he looks at me".

6th Sunday of the Year   *Cycle B*

BE CURED

Things you need

A bell and a bowl (if you have young children in your family).

Prepare your Bible

Old Testament: Leviticus, ch. 13, vv. 1-2, 45-46.
New Testament: St Mark, ch. 1, vv. 40-45.

First Reading

What do you know about leprosy? Have you ever seen or heard an appeal for money to buy the drugs that can cure or at least halt the disease? Have you heard of Father Damien who went out to the leper colony on the island of Molokai to care for the people there? Finally he contracted the disease himself and died of it?

— Any kind of illness was a problem to Moses and his people as they travelled towards the Promised Land. It was essential to have precautions and to organise quarantine regulations. Leprosy was so

H

much feared that rules were particularly strict. How was a leper to warn others that he was approaching?

Ask one of your family to go outside the room (your camp) with his bell and bowl. Let him ring his bell, put down his bowl and go away to a safe distance until his relations inside the camp have put food in his bowl.

Gospel Reading

— When you read this passage and compare it with the first reading you will see that both Jesus and the leper were acting in a very strange way. (See vv. 40, 41.) Yet Jesus asked the man to obey the Jewish law in v. 44. If you are interested you could find out what this offering was by reading Leviticus, ch. 14, vv. 1-32.

— "Of course I want to", said Jesus. Jesus came to make men whole — to heal them in mind and body. There is no one too ill or too ugly or too wicked for Jesus to "touch".

When does Jesus "touch" us?

The prayer over the gifts

Lord,
we make this offering in obedience to your word.
May it cleanse us and renew us,
and lead us to our eternal reward

God gives us so much every day and how little we thank him! Sometimes we are even ungrateful and we grumble and complain. Let us offer ourselves with the bread and wine tomorrow and ask God to accept us and make us more like his Son Jesus.

7th Sunday of the Year   *Cycle B*

LORD, HERE IS OUR FRIEND

Things you need

Draw a section of the house in Capernaum showing the flat roof, the steps outside leading to the roof, the man's friends lowering him down, the man himself halfway down and Jesus with his audience. Make a tiny stretcher with two matchsticks and a piece of cloth or paper.

Prepare your Bible

Old Testament: Isaiah, ch. 43, vv. 18, 19, 21, 22, 24, 25.
New Testament: St Mark, ch. 2, vv. 1-12.

First Reading

Before these verses, Isaiah reminded the Israelites of all God's goodness to them, especially in leading them out of slavery into freedom.
He had brought them to a new life — but how little gratitude they had
shown! Read the passage. Are we sometimes like Jacob in not asking
God to help us?

Are we sometimes like Israel in not bothering about God?

Yet in the Sacrament of Reconciliation, God gives us the way to
come back to him — to ask for his help, to let him take away our
unlovingness and ingratitude so that we, "the people he has formed
for himself", will sing his praises.

Gospel Reading

Let the artist explain his picture before reading.

— Imagine the effort needed to get the paralysed man to Jesus. Build
up the story together starting at the man's house. Do you think
it was his idea or do you think his friends suggested it?

— How can you tell that the five men were sure Jesus would cure
the sick friend?

— Can you think of any example of relatives or friends these days
going out of their way to search for a cure for someone they love?
e.g., pilgrimages, raising money for a special treatment, etc.

Prayer

We can bring people we love to Jesus by our prayer. Let us write the
names of any sick person we know round the picture we have drawn.
Pray for each one, perhaps using a line from the Responsorial Psalm,

e.g. We pray for Uncle David — Lord, help him in his pain.
We pray for John Smith — Lord, help him to persevere with
his treatment.

LOVE AND JOY

Things you need

Something that has been patched. A picture of a wedding.

Prepare your Bible

Old Testament: Hosea, ch. 2, v. 16, 17, 21, 22.
New Testament: St Mark, ch. 2, vv. 18-22.

First Reading

Hosea, like the other prophets, was concerned to bring his people back to love and serve God. They wanted to show how faithful and full of patience was the love of God for his chosen people. In this reading Hosea makes God speak like a husband longing to receive the love of his wife. What moment in Jewish history does he speak of, when the people of God really did respond to God with all their hearts?

How does God show in this passage that he will never desert his people?

Gospel Reading

You remember that John the Baptist came to prepare the people for the coming of Jesus. This involved turning away from sinful lives and learning to control bad habits. This made John appear rather stern and strict with followers.

— John had disciples, the Pharisees had disciples and Jesus had disciples. Give another word for "disciple".

— Jesus compares himself to a bridegroom. His arrival in the world makes life full of joy, like a wedding. Who are his attendants? When will it be time for his attendants to fast?

— Look at the patched sheet or piece of clothing you have found. What would happen if you patched an old sheet with new material?

— Jesus came with news. It needed a new heart to accept it. If we say to ourselves about the Gospel: "I've heard all this before", we will be like the old wineskins which couldn't hold the new wine.

Prayer

Make three little crosses on your forehead, lips and heart as we do before listening to the Gospel. Let us ask God to make us new wineskins, able to hold the message of the Gospel.

9th Sunday of the Year   *Cycle B*

SUNDAY!

Prepare your Bible

Old Testament: Deuteronomy, ch. 5, vv. 12-15.
New Testament: St Mark, ch. 2, vv. 23 to ch. 3, v. 6.

First Reading

The Sabbath day for the Jews begins at sunset on Friday evening and ends at sunset on Saturday. Everything is cleaned, food is prepared for the meals, candlesticks are polished, clean clothes worn. A restful, happy family day is the Sabbath.

— Why is the Sabbath day to be kept holy?
— What can we do to make our Sundays more restful and happy so that they lead us to be holy?

Gospel Reading

Here we have two examples of old skins not being able to hold new wine! The Pharisees expected very exact observance of the Law of Moses.

— Read the passage and then say what law the disciples might have been breaking in picking the ears of corn.
  Thou shalt not . . .
— What Law could Jesus have been breaking when he healed the man with the crippled hand?
  Thou shalt not . . .
— Jesus came to show us that we should live our lives out of love for God — morality is not negative.
— How did Jesus show that he was God by what he said in v. 28?

117

— How does v. 5 show how human Jesus was?

— If today's Gospel was the only description of Jesus, what would we know about his character?

— What effect did this miracle have on the Pharisees?

Prayer

> Lord,
> guide us with your Spirit
> that we may honour you
> not only with our lips
> but also with the lives we lead,
> and so enter your kingdom.

10th Sunday of the Year   *Cycle B*

FRIENDSHIP WITH GOD

Prepare your Bible

Old Testament: Genesis, ch. 3, vv. 9-15.
New Testament: St Mark, ch. 3, vv. 20-35.

First Reading

If we read verse 8, we have a wonderful picture of the way man was completely at home with God — "walking in the garden in the cool of the day".

The story we read gives us the sad fact that the perfect trust and love between God and man was spoiled by disobedience. We do not know exactly how this happened, but we know that we live in a world which has been spoiled by sin and pride and jealousy.

Our hope lies in the redemption brought us by Jesus Christ and there is a little hint in v. 15, that evil will be overcome.

— Who do we Christians understand by "the woman . . . and her offspring?"

Response to the Psalm

> "With the Lord there is mercy
> and fulness of redemption".

Could you talk about this response so that everyone understands it?

Gospel Reading

This reading is in two parts. First we hear how Jesus answered those who tried to say that his miracles were performed through the power of the Devil. What picture does Jesus paint in words to explain how ridiculous this accusation is?

Then vv. 31-35. Jesus seemed to cause anxiety to his relations by the crowds of people he attracted. When the message finally penetrated to him through the crowd, what great lesson did he give to all who were listening to him?

"Anyone who does the will of God". This message is for all time and therefore for us. *Jesus Christ is our brother* if we are trying to live in God's way.

Prayer

Lord,
may your healing love
turn us from sin,
and keep us on the way that leads to you.

11th Sunday of the Year   *Cycle B*

GROWING

Things you need

A few seeds, from different plants if possible — these can be from a packet of seeds or from plants growing round you. Try to remember where you have seen a cedar tree or find a picture of one in a book.

Prepare your Bible

Old Testament: Ezekiel, ch. 17, vv. 22-24.
New Testament: St Mark, ch. 4, vv. 26-34.

First Reading

These verses are part of a poem at the beginning of the chapter which the older members of the family might like to read. The meaning behind this poem is that God will take care of the people he has chosen. In time he will send the Messiah to bring about his kingdom of love.

— v. 22. How does the writer show that the "tree" he is going to plant will be a very specially chosen one?

— v. 23. How does he show that this "tree" is going to be for everybody?

— v. 24. How does he show that everything will be in the loving power of this "tree?"

Response to the Psalm

"It is good to give you thanks, O Lord".

The psalm is about trees. Listen to it carefully at Mass.

Gospel Reading

Look at the seeds you have found. What a power of growth is inside that tiny thing! Tell the rest of your family what it is going to grow into. What seeds from trees do you know? Acorn, apple pip, conker, etc.

Now read the two stories Jesus told as recorded by St Mark. Jesus often used stories to try to explain the Kingdom of God to his disciples. These stories can help us too, to understand how we belong to this kingdom.

— vv. 26-29. We can think how slowly and surely plants grow. Can we say the same about ourselves? We know we grow out of our clothes. We know that suddenly we discover we can swim or understand decimals or logarithms. It is more difficult to know how the seed of faith planted in baptism is growing but we believe that prayer and the sacraments help us to become more like Jesus.

— vv. 30-32. How does this compare with Ezekiel's poem?

Prayer

Almighty God,
our hope and our strength,
without you we falter.
Help us to follow Christ
and to live according to your will.

SAFE IN GOD'S HANDS

Things you need

Paper for each member of the family and pencils and crayons to share. A cushion.

Prepare your Bible

Old Testament: Job, ch. 38, vv. 8-11;
                       Psalm 106 (107), vv. 23-31. Some sailed to the sea
                       in ships.
New Testament: St Mark, ch. 4, vv. 35-41.

First Reading

— "Then from the heart of the tempest" is a phrase used to show God's might and power, and his presence.
— Read the verses from Job and also the Responsorial Psalm. How do they show God's might and power?
— Which verses show God's love and care of his people in danger?
— Draw some pictures to illustrate some of the verses and challenge each other to identify them.

Gospel Reading

Read this incident described by St Mark. See if your pictures can help to illustrate the situation. Re-read the passage, taking parts and acting it. This is why you need a cushion.

Opening prayer of the Mass

    Father,
    guide and protector of your people,
    grant us an unfailing respect for your name,
    and keep us always in your love.

— How does this prayer link up with the readings?
— Could you make up some family Bidding Prayers suitable for the theme of this Sunday's Mass?
    e.g., people in danger,
          people who are afraid —
              before operations? before interviews? before exams? . . .

— Take a few minutes to pray for these people.

Lord, in your mercy, hear our prayer.

Sum up your prayers with the opening prayer of the Mass.

13th Sunday of the Year   *Cycle B*

FULLY ALIVE

Prepare your Bible

Old Testament: Wisdom, ch. 1, vv. 13-15; ch. 2, vv. 23-24.
New Testament: St Mark, ch. 5, vv. 21-43.

First Reading

God created us "TO BE". When do you most feel alive? God created all things GOOD. When do you feel most happy in every part of your being?

Read these verses from the Book of Wisdom. Nothing can destroy the good, God-given part of us. "We believe in life everlasting".

Prayer

Father,
you call your children
to walk in the light of Christ.
Free us from darkness
and keep us in the radiance of your truth.

There can be little "deaths" in ourselves when we sin but Jesus accepted death so that we might be forgiven and live.

Gospel Reading

Jesus came to bring life, to help us "TO BE" the person God created. During his life on earth he often showed his desire and his God-given power to restore life, and to give people the possibility of living fully.

In the miracle of Jairus's daughter, Jesus actually gave life back to the little girl who had died.

— Who was Jairus?

— How old was his daughter?
— Who witnessed the miracle?
— What two things did Jesus tell the witnesses to do?
  In the miracle of the healing of the woman with a haemorrhage,
  Jesus made it possible for her to "live fully". She did not dare to
  ask Jesus to make her better. What did she do?
— How did Jesus know that someone had approached him in faith
  and received his healing power?
— What was the reaction of the disciples when Jesus seemed deter-
  mined to discover who it was?
— What did Jesus say to the woman?
— After which sacraments, which are meetings with Jesus, does the
  priest say to us, "Go in peace?"

Verses from the psalm

> The Lord listened and had pity.
> The Lord came to my help.
> For me you have changed my mourning into dancing,
> O Lord my God, I will thank you for ever.

14th Sunday of the Year   *Cycle B*

LISTEN TO GOD

Prepare your Bible

Old Testament: Ezekiel, ch. 2, vv. 2-5.
New Testament: St Mark, ch. 6, vv. 1-6.

First Reading

Ezekiel was a priest who worked among the exiled Israelites in Babylon
nearly 600 years before Christ. He was a prophet who had visions
to help him understand what God was asking him to do. After the
verses we read today, Ezekiel saw a scroll full of "lamentations, wailings,
moanings," and he was asked to eat this scroll.
— What do you think that vision was meant to tell him?

— From the reading, in what frame of mind were the Israelites in their relationship with God?

— Do you think Ezekiel's work among them was going to be easy?

Gospel Reading

Read the passage together. Jesus was a Jew and he and his disiciples were very faithful in keeping Jewish customs. During the worship in the synagogue on the Sabbath day, visiting preachers would be invited to address the congregation. Many of the congregation would have known Jesus well — they would have been neighbours, customers, childhood friends — so they would have been particularly interested to listen to his sermon.

— They recognised his preaching power and his miracles so why would they not accept him joyfully and proudly?

— The reference to the brothers and sisters of Jesus need not worry us. In Hebrew and Aramaic, more distant relatives were given this title and this is still the custom in Nazareth.

— Why was Jesus able to cure only a few people in his own town? What was absolutely essential if a person wished to be healed by Jesus?

Proclaiming the Gospel today

Before the priest reads the Gospel, you may see him bow towards the altar to pray. This is the prayer he says: "May the Lord be in my heart and on my lips, that I may worthily and fittingly proclaim the Holy Gospel".

As we prepare to listen to the Gospel, we stand and we mark our foreheads, lips and hearts with a cross. Let us ask God that we may always 'accept' his Son Jesus Christ as our Saviour and Lord.

15th Sunday of the Year   *Cycle B*

GO, TELL EVERYONE

Prepare your Bible

Old Testament: Amos, ch. 7, vv. 12-15.
New Testament: St Mark, ch. 6, vv. 7-13.

First Reading

Amos lived about 750 years before Jesus. He was a shepherd but probably looked after cattle as well. Sycamores were a kind of wild fig and his job was to nip the fruit so as to let out the insect which prevented the fig from ripening. God had called Amos from his shepherding to be his prophet and to proclaim an unpopular message in Bethel. There was a great rift between the rich people and the poor. The latter suffered injustice from those who increased their own comfort and luxurious living at the expense of poor people who had no means of redress.

— Why do you think Amos was being sent away from Bethel?

— How did Amos show that he knew he was obeying God?

Gospel Reading

In the Gospel today we read of the way Jesus sent out his disciples as missionaries. We can notice the simple way in which they had to live.

— Did they go out alone?

— Besides what they were actually wearing, what could they take as 'luggage'?

— What were they to do about lodging while they were away from home?

— What was the main message they carried? How did it resemble the preaching of John the Baptist?

— What miraculous powers did Jesus entrust them with?

— What did they use in curing the sick? Is this still used today?

Second Reading

Here are some words from the letter of St Paul to the Ephesians. As confirmed Christians, we are sent out like the disciples to proclaim the Good News. "God chose us, chose us in Christ, . . . to live through love in his presence . . . You too have been stamped with the seal of the Holy Spirit of the Promise . . . to make his glory praised".

Prayer after Communion

Lord,
by our sharing in the mystery of this Eucharist,
let your saving love grow within us.

THE GOOD SHEPHERD

Things you need

A picture of a shepherd with his sheep. The words of a hymn you know based on the 'shepherd' psalm, e.g. 'The King of love my shepherd is' or 'The Lord's my shepherd, I'll not want'.

Prepare you Bible

Old Testament: Jeremiah, ch. 23, vv. 1-6.
New Testament: St Mark, ch. 6, vv. 30-34.

First Reading

This passage helped the Israelites to keep alive the hope that one day God would send his Messiah to rescue them from their unhappiness.

The care with which a shepherd looks after his flock was so well known that it seemed the very best way of describing God's care for his chosen people.

— How does Jeremiah explain that not one of God's own people will be lost?

— 'A virtuous branch for David'. Looking back about 2600 years, to the time when this was written, we can interpret this phrase. Who do we take it to mean?

Sing or say together the hymn you have found. Notice specially the various ways the shepherd takes care of his sheep.

Gospel Reading

These few verses tell us how the disciples returned from the missionary journeys we read about last Sunday. How we wish we could know what they told Jesus!

— How can we tell that they were tired after this first mission?

126

— They were going to have what we might call a 'retreat'. Share with each other what you know about 'making a retreat'.
— But their peaceful day with Jesus was not to be. What happened?
— Jesus could have been disappointed that his plan was spoiled. What did he do?

Opening prayer of the Mass
> Lord,
> be merciful to your people.
> Fill us with your gifts
> and make us always eager to serve you
> in faith, hope, and love.

— Let us look forward to the week to come. Can we foresee the ways we shall be able to serve God? What gifts from God shall we specially need this week?

Remember
The Lord is my shepherd; there is nothing I shall want.

17th Sunday of the Year   *Cycle B*

GOD CAN DO EVERYTHING

Prepare your Bible
Old Testament: 2 Kings, ch. 4, vv. 42-44.
New Testament: St John, ch. 6, vv. 1-15.

First Reading
Read this passage together and see if it reminds you of a similar occasion.

Response to the psalm
> "You open wide your hand, O Lord,
>   and grant our desires".

— What is growing in our gardens and fields at this moment which is a good example of the generosity of God?

Gospel Reading

This is an episode which you thought of when you read of Elisha's miracle.

— Imagine the small boy Andrew found. Can you make up the conversation between him and Andrew before he consented to come to Jesus?

— 'Nothing is impossible to God', and Jesus is God-made-man. He can do wonderful things with us, however little we think we have to offer. The important thing is to be ready to offer ourselves.

Think of what God does with our gifts of bread and wine at Mass. After offering the bread and wine, the priest says quietly:

> Lord God, we ask you to receive us
> and be pleased with the sacrifice we offer you
> with humble and contrite hearts.

— What has happened during this last week that we can offer God at the moment of the offertory — joys, sorrows, good work done for others, pain, beautiful things?

— What can we foresee in this coming week that we can offer to God — something difficult, a party, a sacrifice in order to make someone else happy?

Opening prayer of the Mass

Let us pray that we will make good use of the gifts that God has given us.

> God our Father and protector,
> without you nothing is holy,
> nothing has value.
> Guide us to everlasting life
> by helping us to use wisely
> the blessings you have given to the world.

BREAD FROM HEAVEN

Things you need

A well-written card that you can keep for several weeks: I AM THE BREAD OF LIFE. Your First Communion certificates or medals, etc.

Prepare your Bible

Old Testament: Exodus, ch. 16, vv. 2-4, 12-15.
New Testament: St John, ch. 6, vv. 24-35.

First Reading

This is another example of God's generosity in taking care of his chosen people while they were wandering in the desert. Manna is a sticky substance that comes out of tamarisk trees particularly when stung by an insect. It drips to the ground and hardens overnight. It tastes sweet and is a favourite food for wandering desert tribes.

— The Israelites seemed to have forgotten once again how wonderful it was to be free. Why were they complaining to Moses?

— Although the manna was a natural thing to be found in the desert, Moses had to point it out to the people.

We shall never exhaust the wonders of God which are gradually made known to us through scientists and botanists and musicians etc.

Response to the psalm

"The Lord gave them bread from heaven".

Listen to the psalm on Sunday. The psalmist is recounting the episode of the manna in a poetical way.

Gospel Reading

In this reading, we see how the Jews linked up in their minds the story of the manna with the feeding of the five thousand that we read about last Sunday. Jesus now wants them to go a very big step forwards.

— Choose a narrator, someone to read the part of Jesus and someone to be a spokesman for the people.

We can understand what Jesus was telling them because we live after the Last Supper and after the Resurrection. We know that

129

I

Jesus comes to us under the form of bread in Holy Communion. How difficult it must have been for those Jews to follow what Jesus was trying to lead them to see.

— Look at the card you have prepared. Let us spend a few moments quietly telling Jesus our Lord that we believe what he says.
— Think of the moment of Communion. "The Body of Christ".
— Keep your card for next week. "Amen".

19th Sunday of the Year   *Cycle B*

THE BREAD OF LIFE

Things you need
Your card prepared last week.

Prepare your Bible
Old Testament:
    1 Kings, ch. 19, vv. 4-8.
New Testament:
    St John, ch. 6, vv. 41-51.

First Reading
Elijah had been banished by Queen
Jezebel. He was feeling downcast
and hopeless as he wandered like a fugitive on his 300 mile pilgrimage to try to safeguard faith in the one true God.

— How can we tell he was giving up hope in himself?
— What signs did God choose to give him courage and confidence to go on?

Response to the psalm
    "Taste and see that the Lord is good".
— How does this response seem to fit the reading about Elijah?
— Listen to the verses of the psalm on Sunday and see if these fit the story as well.

Gospel Reading
Put your card so that everyone can see it.

— Why did the Jews object to what Jesus said about himself?

— How did Jesus try to explain that this Bread is quite different from the manna their ancestors ate?

— "The bread that I shall give is my flesh, for the life of the world". This makes the 'giving' sound like a sacrifice and we know that the death of Jesus was just that. We speak about the 'Sacrifice of the Mass' during which the priest at the consecration says: "Take this, all of you, and eat it. This is my body which will be given up for you".

Consider the Preface for the Mass of Corpus Christi

In this great sacrament you feed your people
and strengthen them in holiness,
so that the family of mankind
may come to walk in the light of one faith,
in one communion of love.
We come then to this wonderful sacrament
to be fed at your table
and grow into the likeness of the risen Christ.

Let us pause for a moment and ask that each time we receive Jesus, the Bread of life, we may become a little more like him.

20th Sunday of the Year   *Cycle B*

THE LIVING BREAD

Things you need

Your card 'I AM THE BREAD OF LIFE'.

Prepare your Bible

Old Testament: Proverbs, ch. 9, vv. 1-6.
New Testament: Ephesians, ch. 5, vv. 15-20;
          St John, ch. 6, vv. 51-58.

First Reading

We can think of many proverbs in our own culture and language. Speaking in proverbs was a popular way of communicating wise sayings. In the reading from the book of Proverbs wisdom is seen as a person. If we understand that 'wisdom' is taken to mean 'God', how do these verses tell us that God welcomes everyone, no matter how poor or ignorant he may be?

Response to the psalm
"Taste and see that the Lord is good".
Why is this a good response to follow the reading from Proverbs?

Second Reading
— It has been said that 'he who sings to God, prays twice'. What do you think about that?
— What does St Paul advise the Christians of Ephesus to do in order to thank God always?
— Do you ever have a song or a tune that you can't get out of your head? If it can be a song of joy and praise, what a marvellous prayer it can be!

Gospel Reading
The greatest prayer of thanksgiving to God is the Eucharist. The Gospel passage today is once again about Jesus, the living bread.
— When you have read through the whole passage together, go back to the beginning and read out each phrase which contains the the words — life, living, live.
— We can see how important the Eucharist is for giving us life if Jesus spoke about it so often. Take each phrase you have noticed, read them slowly again leaving a pause to say in your heart, 'Lord, I believe'.

Breaking the bread

While we say 'Lamb of God' before Holy Communion, the priest takes the Host, breaks it in half and drops a tiny fraction into the chalice while he says this prayer:

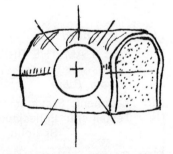

> May this mingling of the body and blood of Our Lord Jesus Christ bring eternal life to us who receive it.

We are asking God for eternal life with him when we receive Holy Communion. We could watch the priest doing this action at Mass on Sunday.

ETERNAL LIFE

Things you need

The leader for this week should go round the house noticing all the signs there are that your family believes in God. (Crucifix, pictures, statues, etc.) Before you start your Bible study together, you could make up a quiz, perhaps taking each room at a time.

Prepare your Bible

Old Testament: Joshua, ch. 24, vv. 1-2, 15-18.
New Testament: St John, ch. 6, vv. 60-69.

First Reading

Joshua was nearing the end of his life. He had led the Israelites into the Promised Land, conquered enemy tribes, and established peace. In this reading we hear how he encouraged the people to choose the one true God as their God for ever.

— What choices did he give them?
— What was he himself determined to do whatever their choice?
— What governed the choice of the people?
— Why did they choose to serve the Lord?

Gospel Reading

This is the fifth Sunday we have been studying the sixth chapter of St John. We have seen how hard the Jews found it to accept the teaching of Jesus. We too may find it hard to accept his teaching and we cannot understand completely the doctrine of the Eucharist, but *we have been given faith to believe it.*

— Some of the *disciples* left Jesus and stopped going with him. What is another word for disciple?
— Did Jesus try to make his teaching easy so that they would not go away? Why?
— Jesus questioned the Twelve. Look carefully at Peter's answer. As we saw last week, it is Jesus who gives us eternal *life.*

Opening prayer of the Mass

We know that when people are all searching for the same thing, they are drawn together in sharing the same desire. The Eucharist is the greatest source of unity there is.

Father,
help us to seek the values
that will bring us enduring joy
in this changing world.
In our desire for what you promise
make us one in mind and heart.

22nd Sunday of the Year   *Cycle B*

HELPS TO HAPPINESS

Prepare your Bible

Old Testament: Deuteronomy, ch. 4, vv. 1-2, 6-8.
New Testament: St Mark, ch. 7, vv. 1-8, 14-15, 21-23.

First Reading

— Very often in Old Testament times, God was considered to be far away from his people and to be feared. However in v. 7 Moses is declaring quite the opposite. What does he say?

— Sometimes we think of laws and rules as being restrictive. What does Moses say about the laws and customs which are given by God? v. 1.

— God made us to know him, love him and serve him in this life and to be happy with him for ever in the next. Why, then, are his laws sure to make us 'wise and prudent'?

Gospel Reading

Moses had said that nothing was to be added to nor taken away from the laws God had given. Read the Gospel passage and discover one activity in life that the Pharisees seemed to have carried to excess.

— We wash our hands before meals. There are stringent regulations in food shops and restaurants about cleanliness. It wasn't this that Jesus was criticising. He called the Pharisees 'hypocrites' and this gives us the clue. Read the quotation from Isaiah (vv. 6, 7) and find out what Jesus meant.

— Can you think of some examples to illustrate what Jesus was teaching? e.g., A mechanic comes into the office, his hands covered with oil and wearing dirty overalls; an office worker in a spotless suit hastily pockets a long strip of Green Shield stamps: 'the last customer didn't want them', he said untruthfully. Which of these two would Jesus call 'unclean'?

To think about

We often say things, think things, and act in a way that makes us 'unclean'. We know we can turn to the God who is so close to us, to ask for forgiveness and for strength to be more like Jesus. Receiving the bread of life often is the best way to do this.

Prayer after Communion

Lord,
you renew us at your table with the bread of life.
May this food strengthen us in love
and help us to serve you in each other.

23rd Sunday of the Year   **Cycle B**

THE WONDERS OF GOD

Things you need

Try to find a few pictures of people who are obviously rich and of people who are poor, either through lack of money or health or friends.

Prepare your Bible

Old Testament: Isaiah, ch. 35, vv. 4-7.
New Testament: James, ch. 2, vv. 1-5;
                St Mark, ch. 7, vv. 31-37.

First Reading

In this reading we are shown what a difference it makes to know God.
— What comparison does Isaiah use in v. 7? For the Jews who spent so much of their lives wandering in the desert, water meant *life*.
— vv. 5, 6 could refer to physical healing which Jesus was to bring

to many people. It can refer, too, to our reception of the Word of God — how can we be blind to God's message?
how can we be deaf to his word?
how can we be lame in his service?
how can we be dumb in his praise?
Let us ask for forgiveness and for healing.

Second Reading

Look at the pictures you have collected and read St James' criticism of the way we sometimes make a difference in the way we treat various people.

Gospel Reading

— How does this miracle of Jesus link up with the verses from Isaiah that we have just read?

— We can wonder what was the first thing the man said.

— 'Their admiration was unbounded'. God still works wonderful things. How much do we admire him? If we think of this miracle, we can also think of the wonders of deaf-aids, the apparatus to help deaf people to speak and the speech-therapist and surgeons who help people with deformities and difficulties connected with speech.

Prayer

Let us spend a few moments quietly thanking God for the gifts of hearing and speech which we take so much for granted.

24th Sunday of the Year   *Cycle B*

THE SAVIOUR

Things you need

A crucifix.

Prepare your Bible

Old Testament: Isaiah, ch. 50, vv. 5-9.
New Testament: St Mark, ch. 8, vv. 27-35.

First Reading

The Jews, who were awaiting the Messiah, would find it difficult to realise that these verses accurately portray him. We, knowing about the suffering and death of Jesus, can wonder anew that God's own Son should have to suffer like this for us.

— How does Isaiah show the meekness and humility of the Messiah?
— What words show the unfailing trust that the Messiah will have in Almighty God?

Response to the psalm

"I will walk in the presence of the Lord in the land of the living". Listen on Sunday to the verses of the psalm and notice how they echo the sentiments of the first reading.

Gospel Reading

This is a very important incident in the disciples' relationship with Jesus. Everyone was wondering who Jesus was. Because the Jews had a good knowledge of the Scriptures, some of them thought that he was one of the prophets who had returned.

— Which prophets were mentioned?
— Peter was the spokesman and declared his conviction.
  What did he say?
— As soon as Peter had professed his faith that Jesus was the anointed one, the Messiah, Jesus was able to start to prepare his disciples for what lay in store for him.
  What sufferings did he mention?
— When Peter would not accept this conception of the Messiah, what did Jesus say to him?
— Jesus went still further. Not only was he to suffer and die, but . . . vv. 34, 35.

  To be a friend and follower of Jesus, it is necessary to keep close to him, and to be willing to become like him. Holy Communion is the gift of Jesus himself.

Prayer after Communion

Lord,
may this Eucharist you have given us
influence our thoughts and actions.
May your Spirit guide and direct us in your way.

TO BE LIKE JESUS

Things you need

A crucifix. A picture of a small child.

Prepare your Bible

Old Testament: Wisdom, ch. 2, vv. 12, 17-20.
New Testament: St Mark, ch. 9, vv. 30-37.

First Reading

We can read these verses with Jesus in mind.
— v. 12. Which group of people felt this way about Jesus?
— vv. 19, 20. How did these things come true?

Response to the psalm

"The Lord upholds my life".

Listen to the verses of the psalm at Mass and see how they help us
to think along the lines of the first reading.

Gospel Reading

"After leaving the mountain" — three of the disciples had just witnessed the glory of Jesus and heard God the Father's voice proclaiming
that Jesus was his beloved Son.
— v. 31. What does Jesus tell his disciples to counterbalance the
wonder of their experience?
Did the disciples understand him?
What do you think was the most difficult part of his teaching —
the announcement of his death or of his resurrection?
— The disciples were very ordinary men and they were as slow as we
are to understand the thoughts of Jesus.
vv. 33, 34. Try to imagine the conversation that had taken place
amongst the disciples on their way to Capernaum.
v. 35. How patient Jesus was with his friends!
v. 37. How did he explain his "Way?"

There is a saying, "He who gives in, wins". In an argument, we find it very difficult to be the one who gives in. It takes a strong, loving, mature nature to be able to give in. Can you think of any examples from home or school life?

Prayer

Let us pray that we will grow in the love of God and of one another.

Father,
guide us, as you guide creation
according to your law of love.
May we love one another
and come to perfection
in the eternal life prepared for us.

26th Sunday of the Year   *Cycle B*

ENTERING THE KINGDOM

Prepare your Bible

Old Testament: Numbers, ch. 11, vv. 25-29.
New Testament: St Mark, ch. 9, vv. 38-43, 45, 47-48.

First Reading

In the Old Testament, the presence of God was often signified by a cloud which "overshadowed" the people to whom God was going to speak. The Tent or Tabernacle was the place where the precious "Law" was kept. Moses was unable to do all the work necessary by himself so we hear how God appointed seventy other people to help him. To prophesy means to act and speak in the name of God, on his authority.
— vv. 27, 28. Why do you think Joshua resented Eldad and Medad prophesying?
— vv. 29, 30. What did Moses feel about the two men?

Gospel Reading

Here we have a parallel case of the disciples resenting someone who did not seem to be "one of us".

— v. 39, 40. How does Jesus reply?

Now comes a very serious warning from Jesus. To be a citizen of the Kingdom of Heaven is the greatest prize to be won. To prevent anyone entering the Kingdom is the worst offence anyone can commit.

— v. 41. How easy is it to be recognised as a friend of Jesus and so to gain entry into his Kingdom?

— v. 42. How serious is it to destroy someone's faith?

— vv. 43-47. How serious is the sin which will prevent a person accepting God's love and living in his Kingdom?

Opening prayer of the Mass

We all sin at times but we are sure of God's desire that we should repent and so receive his forgiveness.

Father,
you show your almighty power
in your mercy and forgiveness.
Continue to fill us with your gifts of love.
Help us to hurry toward the eternal life you promise
and come to share in the joys of your kingdom.

— We often pray: Thy kingdom come. What do we mean?

27th Sunday of the Year   *Cycle B*

MAN, WOMAN AND CHILD

Things you need

Pictures or photos of as many families as you can find.

Prepare your Bible

Old Testament: Genesis, ch. 2, vv. 18-24.
New Testament: St Mark, ch. 10, vv. 2-16.

First Reading

This is part of the second account of creation and it emphasizes the importance of man in comparison with the animals.

140

— v. 18. We are not made to be lonely.

— vv. 19, 20. Name-giving was considered a mark of ownership. Think of some examples of the way man rules animals.

— vv. 21-24. This very solemn picture was calculated to show the Jews that woman was a wonderful complement to man, equal in dignity so that the two could love each other deeply and completely. Talk of some of the ways in which men and women complement each other, e.g., in strength, understanding, gentleness, imagination, etc.

Gospel Reading

The Pharisees were continually trying to find some way of making Jesus deny the Jewish Law. In fact, the *Law of Moses* allowed divorce if there were sufficient grounds. As usual, Jesus goes further than the Law, instead of denying it. He came to perfect the Law, not to destroy it.

— v. 9. What does Jesus say about marriage?

In our Old Testament reading we say that women were made of equal status with men. In vv. 11, 12, we see how a woman can be sinned against in the matter of adultery whereas by Jewish Law this was not considered.

— vv. 13-16. We cannot tell why the disciples were trying to keep the children away from Jesus. What matters is the teaching of Jesus concerning the Kingdom of God.

— What qualities in a small child do you most admire? e.g., joy, truthfulness . . .

God is our Father and we are his children. How does he want us to behave towards him?

— How can we tell that Jesus loved children and valued them?

Prayer

There are many children who are not valued and treasured by their families. Can we pray for them?

TRUE WISDOM

Things you need
Pencil and paper

Prepare your Bible
Old Testament: Wisdom, ch. 7, vv. 7-11.
New Testament: St Mark, ch. 10, vv. 17-30.

First Reading
— When you have read this passage, make a list of all the things Solomon counted as being worth less than wisdom.

— How was it that Solomon was given this great gift?

— To the Jews, wisdom was looked upon as a sign of God's closeness to them. We too can marvel at the wisdom of many people today, including doctors, scientists, theologians, etc. This leads us to realise that all wisdom stems from God the creator. He is the source of all wisdom and we can pray, like Solomon, that we may receive this gift of the Spirit.

Prayer of the Mass
> Lord, our help and our guide,
> make your love the foundation of our lives.
> May our love for you express itself
> in our eagerness to do good for others.

In the psalm
Listen for the verse: "that we may gain wisdom of heart".

Gospel Reading
Read this passage in parts. (The leader should decide how to allot the parts before the family meets.)

— Why do you think the young man asked this question?

— "Jesus looked steadily at him and loved him". If Jesus loved him, why did he ask him to do something so difficult?

— Can you think of any examples today which are like this young man's situation?

— v. 26. What apparently exaggerated example does Jesus use to show how difficult it is for a rich man to enter the kingdom of heaven?

— What is the connection between this reading and the passage from Wisdom?

— vv. 28-31. We see that Jesus does not hide the fact that to be his friend and follower entails hardship in this world, as well as reward and happiness.

Prayer after Communion

Think about this prayer in connection with the last verses of the Gospel, before you pray it together.

> Almighty Father,
> may the body and blood of your Son
> give us a share in his life,
> for he is Lord for ever and ever.

29th Sunday of the Year   *Cycle B*

THE SUFFERING SERVANT

Prepare your Bible

Old Testament: Isaiah, ch. 53, vv. 10-11.
New Testament: Hebrews, ch. 4, vv. 14-16.
                      St Mark, ch. 10, vv. 35-45.

First Reading

This is another description of the Messiah who is coming to suffer in order to save us.

— Take each sentence in turn and see how Jesus fits this picture painted by Isaiah.

Second Reading

As we read this passage, perhaps more than once, we can see how it inspires confidence and trust in Jesus Christ.

Gospel Reading

Once again, the disciples, in the persons of James and John, showed how far they were from understanding the way a friend of Jesus must live.

Jesus asked if they were ready to be bathed in suffering. When they said they were, Jesus accepted their assurance but he was dependent on his Father for their second request. What was this?

— The other disciples showed they understood little more than James and John because they were indignant that the two brothers had thought of asking for such a favour!

— How did Jesus explain the way that a Christian with authority must live?

— Why would the disciples find that the idea of being "slave to all" was difficult ot understand?

— How do our bishops and priests serve us?

— v. 45. Jesus came to carry his service of others to the utmost limit by giving his life. Can you think of people who "give their lives" in various ways for the sake of others?

Prayer

Let us pray for the gift of simplicity and joy in our service of God and man.

Almighty and ever-living God,
our source of power and inspiration,
give us strength and joy
in serving you as followers of Christ,
who lives and reigns with you and the Holy Spirit,
one God, for ever and ever.

FAITH AGAIN

Prepare your Bible

Old Testament: Jeremiah, ch. 31, vv. 7-9.
New Testament: St Mark, ch. 10, vv. 46-52.

First Reading

— "Proclaim, praise, shout!" Why was Jeremiah so excited?
— Complete these phrases to show how God might talk about his people today.

> I will bring them back..................
> I will gather them.......................
> I will comfort them ....
> I will guide them ....

— FOR I AM A FATHER TO ISRAEL. We say, "Our Father" many times. Do we live in the presence of our loving Father and turn to him easily in prayer? Because Jesus is our brother, God looks on us, each one of us, as his beloved son or daughter.

Gospel Reading

Read this passage in parts. Act it if you like.

— Why do you think the people round about the blind man tried to stop him shouting?
— Had they understood the concern Jesus has for everyone, without exception?
— 'He jumped up". Do you think he usually moved so fast?
— How do we know that the man had not always been blind?
— "Go, your faith has saved you". Always Jesus required faith. How had the man showed his faith?
— When we go to Mass, how do we:—

> *show* our faith?
> *declare* our faith?
> *strengthen* our faith?

J

Prayer

Almighty and ever-living God,
strengthen our faith, hope and love.
May we do with loving hearts
what you ask of us
and come to share the life you promise.

— Let us think for a moment of anything we know God is asking of us today.
Let us say the prayer again with this in mind.

31st Sunday of the Year   *Cycle B*

ONE GOD

Prepare your Bible

Old Testament: Deuteronomy, ch. 6, vv. 2-6.
New Testament: St Mark, ch. 12, vv. 28-34.

First Reading

— How does Moses explain to the people that loving and serving the only true God is the sure way to happiness?
— v. 6. Would these words of Moses have the same force if he had said: "Let them be written on your brain or on your memory?"
— These verses are the opening words of the "Shema" which is a great Jewish prayer. The belief in only one God was vital to the Jews, surrounded as they were by tribes and people who had abundant gods to worship.
— What is the first line of the Creed we say on Sunday?

Gospel Reading

— Jesus was a practising Jew and the Shema was part of his prayer. Once again we see that Jesus did not come to renounce the Jewish Law but to deepen and perfect it. What does Jesus add to the words spoken by Moses?
— The Scribes who had asked the question, seemed to accept the answer Jesus gave with an open heart. Certainly some Scribes and

Pharisees became disciples of Jesus. They were not all opposed to him.

— Can you think of some situations in the world today which would improve if these commandments were kept?

Family Prayer

Spend a few moments in quiet prayer after someone has read, one at a time, the two commandments:—

1. You must love the Lord your God with all your heart, with all your mind and with all your strength.
2. You must love your neighbour as yourself.

— Complete your silent prayer by saying the "Our Father" together slowly.

32nd Sunday of the Year   *Cycle B*

GENEROSITY

Things you need

A small dish of flour, a jug of water, a knob of butter or margarine, two half-penny pieces, the largest piece of paper money you can borrow.

Prepare your Bible

Old Testament: 1 Kings, ch. 17, vv. 10-16.
New Testament: St Mark, ch. 12, vv. 38-44.

First Reading

It was a time of drought and all the rivers and streams had run dry. Elijah, the prophet, was led by God to ask help of a widow who lived in Sidon, a part of the country despised by practising Jews.

— What corresponds in the story to the things you have put on the table?

— Ask your mother how to make scones or look up the recipe.

— Prophets, men of God, were revered by ordinary people who were glad to help them. However, in this desperate situation so near to death, the woman needed reassurance. Read together the promise Elijah voiced on behalf of God.

147

— It is often the poorest people who are the most generous. Do you agree and can you give any examples?

Gospel Reading
— What signs of "showing-off" does Jesus mention?
— v. 40. What makes this "showing-off" even worse?
— vv. 41-44. What a contrast to the last few verses! And how similar to Elijah's experience with the widow in Sidon! The coins given by this widow were worth less than the two halfpenny pieces you have found.
— In actual material value, which gift was the most worthwhile for the Temple treasury, to provide doves, incense, etc.?
— Why then does Jesus praise her so highly?
— If we think of radio or television appeals for Good Causes, some of the money that is raised is sent by Old Age Pensioners. Why do you think they respond to appeals as generously as they can? Could there be a temptation to think that because they can only spare a small sum, it is not worth sending it?
— What does the expression "It's the thought that counts" mean?
— Could we consider the money we put into the collection at Mass? Is it realistic for each one of us?

Prayer ofer the gifts
> God of mercy,
> in this eucharist we proclaim the death of the Lord.
> Accept the gifts we present
> and help us to follow him with love,
> for he is Lord for ever and ever.

33rd Sunday of the Year   *Cycle B*

SIGNS OF THE TIMES

Prepare your Bible
Old Testament: Daniel, ch. 12, vv. 1-3.
New Testament: St Mark, ch. 13, vv. 24-32.

First Reading

The book of Daniel was written to encourage the Jews in their hope of salvation. Michael was their patron angel and he was going to take care of them during the terrible times that were coming.
— Which verse refers to the resurrection of the body?
— v. 3. Can you think of some saints to whom this verse could apply?

Gospel Reading

As this is the last Sunday of the Church's year, we can see why this Gospel reading has been chosen, together with the passage from Daniel.
— vv. 24-27. Jesus speaks of frightening signs but also of a wonderful sign. What will the Son of Man send his angels to do?
— A parable is a story with a hidden meaning. Watching the trees is one of the ways we have of recognising the seasons. There will be signs to tell us that the end of the world is near.
— v. 32. What can we think of the sects who prophesy certain dates for the end of the world?

Prayer

Let us pray that God will help us to be faithful in trying to love him and serve him, believing that he has us all safe in his keeping.

Father of all that is good,
keep us faithful in serving you,
for to serve you is our lasting joy.

We believe

that Jesus will come again in glory to judge the living and the dead,
and his kingdom will have no end.
We look for the resurrection of the dead,
and the life of the world to come.
— We say this every Sunday. It is good to think about it before we say it next time.

Christ the King — see page 82

Cycle C

CONFIDENCE

Things you need

An Advent wreath (see page 14). Prepare a little part of your family tree, just as far as your grandparents.

Prepare your Bible

Old Testament: Jeremiah, ch. 33, vv. 14-16.
New Testament: St Luke, ch. 21, vv. 25-28, 34-36.

First Reading

Read the pasage from Jeremiah. What promise did God make to his chosen people, the Israelites?

Look at the family tree you have started. Can you see a branch of your family? Perhaps a branch has settled in Australia . . . perhaps a branch has strayed in Ireland. In the reading God says: "I will make a virtuous Branch grow for David". Who was God referring to?

Next time you have a hymn book, look up "O come, O come, Emmanuel" and find out the verse which refers to David.

Gospel Reading

Light the first candle of your Advent wreath. You could say as you light it:

> "May the coming of Jesus Christ bring us the light of his holiness".

Advent is the time when we think about the coming of Jesus in glory at the end of time. Sometimes we call it his Second Coming.

Who do you think will be afraid when this time approaches?

There is no need for us to fear, crouched down and shaking. How are we to stand?

BUT we have to be ready and steadily prepare ourselves for that mysterious day.

"Stay awake," says Jesus, "and pray at all times".

A resolution for Advent

Let us think about our night prayers. Could we pray together each night? If we pray alone, could we be sure to kneel down, at least to make the Sign of the Cross before jumping into our warm bed.

WALK IN SAFETY

Things you need

Your Advent wreath. If you have young children in your family — an old dark dress, a pretty dress, something to wear as a cloak and a crown made from a strip of cardboard and silver paper. Find out the East and West direction of the room you will be working in.

Prepare your Bible

Old Testament: Baruch, ch. 5, vv. 1-9.
New Testament: St Luke, ch. 3, vv. 1-6.

First Reading

Read this together first and decide how you will act it. Have a chair ready to stand on. Decide how you can show verse 6.

How is God going to take care of his chosen people, Israel? How will he guide them? What is an escort?

You could light your first Advent candle when you read "by the light of his glory".

To think about

Jerusalem was a very special city to the Jews because it contained the Temple.

We are thinking at this time of the year of the coming of Jesus to save us. What happened to Jesus in Jerusalem that brought our salvation?

New Testament

Write down the names of the important people mentioned in vv. 1 and 2. Some of them were concerned with government and some with religion. God did not choose them to prepare the way for his Son.

Where did John the Baptist live when God told him what he was to do?

Take the phrases from Isaiah and discover how they can be symbols of what we need to do to prepare for the coming of Christ at Christmas.

Prepare a way — celebrate the Sacrament of Reconciliation, perhaps.

Every valley shall be filled in — no "being down in the dumps?"
Every mountain and hill be laid low — try to be less proud?
Winding ways will be straightened — try to tell the truth?
Rough roads made smooth — the way we speak to each other?

Prayer

Let us pray that nothing may hinder us from receiving Christ with joy.
(Pause.) Our Father . . .

3rd Sunday of Advent   *Cycle C*

A TIME FOR JOY

Things you need

Your Advent wreath. Christmas cards received so far. A way of demon-
strating winnowing to young members of the family.

Prepare your Bible

New Testament: Philippians, ch. 4, vv. 4-7.
                St Luke, ch. 3, vv. 10-18.

First Reading

Light three candles before you begin. When you have read this text,
discuss the following:

   What made you happy when you were a few months old?
   What made you happy when you were ten years old?
   What will make your Christmas happy this year?
   What plans have you made to make other people happy?
   What is the key to happiness that you gradually find as you
       grow older?

Gospel Reading

Choose someone to be John the Baptist, the ordinary people, tax collectors, soldiers and a narrator.

   What kind of picture of Jesus does John give by his example of the treatment of wheat? John was trying to impress on his listeners the need to live good lives.

Prayer

Share out your Christmas cards and take it in turn to pray for the senders. St Paul said in his letter that "if there is anything you need, pray for it".

Think of the people who have sent you cards and pray for any special needs they have.

E.g. This card is from Uncle Bill. He's out of work, isn't he? Let's ask God to lead him to find a job.

4th Sunday of Advent   *Cycle C*

A TIME FOR PEACE

Things you need

Your Advent wreath. Your rosaries.

Prepare your Bible

Old Testament: Micah, ch. 5, vv. 1-4.
New Testament: St Luke, ch. 1, vv. 39-44.

First Reading

Where does Micah foretell that the Messiah will be born?

How does he hint that the Messiah will come as a baby and not with the show of power and glory that the Jews expected?

"He will extend his power to the ends of the Land". What was our Lord's last command to his disciples that links up with this verse?

"He himself will be peace". What title do we give to Jesus in "Hark the herald angels sing" which links up with this verse?

Preface for the second part of Advent

Father, all-powerful and ever-living God,
we do well always and everywhere to give you thanks
through Jesus Christ our Lord.

His future coming was proclaimed by all the prophets (name three).
The virgin mother bore him in her womb with love beyond all telling.
John the Baptist was his herald
and made him known when at last he came. (How and Where?)
In his love Christ has filled us with joy
as we prepare to celebrate his birth,
so that when he comes he may find us watching in prayer,
our hearts filled with wonder and praise.

Gospel Reading

"Wonder and praise". Do you think this would describe the feelings of Elizabeth?

The visit of Mary to Elizabeth is the picture we contemplate in the second Joyful Mystery of the Rosary. We can let our mind run over the incidents — Mary travelling in the countryside, arriving at Elizabeth's house, the two cousins embracing each other, looking at each other with love and reverence knowing what God had done for both of them.

Gathered round your Advent wreath with its four candles and no other light, say this decade of the Rosary together. You can share rosaries if you haven't one each.

Sunday in the Octave of Christmas — see page 18

2nd Sunday after Christmas — see page 19

Sunday after Epiphany — see page 20

1st Sunday of Lent   *Cycle C*

ON THE WAY TO EASTER

Things you need

One of your best saucers or a glass dish with the money for the collection you are going to give on Sunday. A flower or twig with new leaves showing. Your crucifix.

Prepare your Bible

Old Testament: Deuteronomy, ch. 26, vv. 4-10.
New Testament: St Luke, ch. 4, vv. 1-13.

First Reading

Read how the Jews always remembered the way God had rescued them from slavery and brought them through many trials into a land of freedom.

— How were the Jews to show their gratitude to God?

— Put your flower or twig and your collection by your crucifix.

It is too early in the year in this country to have produce from the garden, but let us thank God for the signs of life in the world.

Have you seen any lambs yet?

What bulbs are flowering?

Are buds swelling on the fruit trees?

Our collection at Mass is a "sign" of our "thank you" to God.

Prayer over the gifts

Lord,
make us worthy to bring you these gifts.
(What other gifts do we offer at Mass?)
May this sacrifice
help to change our lives.
(What changes are we asking for this Lent?)

Gospel Reading

This important event in the life of Jesus followed his baptism by John in the Jordan. Jesus was making the last stage of his preparation for the work his Father had sent him to do in the world. This last stage was a retreat. Have any of your family made a retreat?

— Where did Jesus go for his retreat?

— How long did it last?

— Jesus had taken no food all that time. He must have been weak with hunger. This was the most difficult moment of the retreat. Surrounded by the flat stones of the desert, how was Jesus tempted to use his power to make life easier for himself?

— How was Jesus tempted to turn from God's plan in order to have power and possessions?

— How was Jesus tempted to win people to him by showing off?

2nd Sunday of Lent   *Cycle C*

WONDERFUL SIGNS

Things you need

Draw outlines of a heifer, a goat, a ram, a turtledove and a pigeon as if you are looking down on them. A tiny tray or baking dish, a pair of scissors, matches and a taper.

Prepare your Bible

Old Testament: Genesis, ch. 15, vv. 5-12, 17-18.
New Testament: St Luke, ch. 9, vv. 28-36.

First Reading

You remember how Abram left his country in order to follow God's call. God had promised him a country and many descendants. How many? v. 5. This seemed impossible to Abram who, as yet, had not a single child. He asked God for a sign that the land would be his.

— Read the passage. Cut your animals in half and arrange them on a tray.

— Light your taper and make it pass between the two lines of carcasses. Act Abram driving off the birds of prey.

This fire passing through, stood for God himself as he was making a solemn pact or covenant with Abram. In the days of Abram this was the way to make an agreement with someone but usually only one animal was needed. The two parties walked between the dead carcass, promising they would keep the agreement and showing that if they did not keep it, the fate of the animal would be theirs.

— What was the Covenant that God was making with Abram?

159

Prayer

In the Gospel we read of another sign of God's presence.
Let us ask God to help us to listen to his Word.

> God our Father,
> help us to hear your Son.
> Enlighten us with your word,
> that we may find the way to your glory.

Gospel Reading

Read St Luke's account of the Transfiguration of Jesus.

— Why did Jesus go up the mountain?
— Do you think the light shone *on* Jesus or do you think it seemed to come from *within* him?
— What were Moses and Elijah talking to Jesus about?
— Very often a cloud was the sign of the presence of God to the Jews. What did Peter and James and John hear?
— "The disciples kept silence". What do you think they were feeling?

A moment's silence with Jesus, not on the mountain top, but in our home.

3rd Sunday of Lent   ***Cycle C***

GOD CARES FOR US

Things you need

A special place to put your Bible in your really tidy room! Write, large enough for everyone to see, "The Lord is compassion and love". Put it where it can be seen as you work together.

Prepare your Bible

Old Testament: Exodus, ch. 3, vv. 1-8, 13-15.
New Testament: St Luke, ch. 13, vv. 1-9.

First Reading

You could ask someone to read the part of Moses and someone to read the words of God.

— Moses was working when God chose to speak to him. How did God attract his attention?
— How was Moses told to show respect for the place where he was meeting God?
— Do you know any religion which continues this custom?
— How do Catholics show respect for God's house?
— The Jews attached very great importance to the name of a person. What was the name God told Moses to use when speaking of him?
— How was God going to show his compassion and love for his people?

Gospel Reading
Read the parable that Jesus told vv. 6-9. Have you ever had this experience with a plant? Have you ever said: "Let's wait another few days and see if anything happens?"
— In the story there are two men — the owner of the vineyard and the man who worked there. Which was the man who wanted to give the vine another chance? Why do you think it was he who had the most patience?
— What is Jesus trying to help us to understand about his care for us?
— Now go back to verse 1. Here Jesus is giving us a warning. "Unless you repent". Jesus is full of kindness and patience but if we have understood his "Good News", then he expects us to live by it. This means continually coming back to him and learning to be more like him.

Prayer

Let us think for a moment about the way we are keeping our Lent resolutions . . . . and pray for confidence in the love of God and the strength to overcome our weakness.

Father,
you have taught us to overcome our sins
by prayer, fasting and works of mercy.
When we are discouraged by our weakness,
give us confidence in your love. Amen.

K

HALF WAY AND MOTHER'S DAY!

Things you need

If possible a picture from a newspaper of people meeting after a long separation, e.g., after a journey, being released from prison, leaving hospital, etc.

Prepare your Bible

Old Testament: Joshua, ch. 5, vv. 9-12.
New Testament: 2 Corinthians, ch. 5, vv. 17-21.
St Luke, ch. 15, vv. 1-3, 11-32.

Opening Prayer

Father of peace,
we are joyful in your Word,
your Son Jesus Christ,
who reconciles us to you.
Let us hasten towards Easter
with the eagerness of faith and love.

First Reading

Here we read how the Israelites at last reached the Promised Land. When they had pitched their tents, what did they celebrate? . . . They remembered and celebrated God's goodness. How did their food change once they were in Canaan?

Second Reading

There are some lovely phrases in this reading:
— For anyone who is in Christ, there is a new creation.
— We are ambassadors for Christ.
— Be reconciled to God.
— . . . in him we might become the goodness of God.
This Sunday is a special day of joy to cheer us on our way through Lent. The priest may wear pink vestments at Mass and there may be flowers on the altar. In our family we pay special attention to our mother and try to make the day a happy one. How do the phrases we have selected lead us to happiness?

162

Gospel Reading

As we read the parable today, we might think especially of the father in the story.

— What do you think he felt when he saw his young son leaving home?

— How do you think he thought about the boy every single day he was missing?

— How often do you think he looked down the road in the hope of seeing the boy on his way back home?

— What signs without words showed his joy when the boy came home at last?

— What kind of celebration did he arrange?

— How did he try to explain to the older son the reason for rejoicing?

Prayer

> Father,
> fill our hearts with the light of your Gospel,
> that our thoughts may please you
> and our love be sincere.

5th Sunday of Lent   *Cycle C*

WE SHALL OVERCOME

Things you need

Your crucifix. A cup or medal or certificate won for sport or gymnastics.

Prepare your Bible

Old Testament: Isaiah, ch. 43, vv. 16-21.
New Testament: Philippians, ch. 3, vv. 8-14.
                        St John, ch. 8, vv. 1-11.

First Reading

We are approaching Passover time for the Jews. We are approaching too the celebration of the events when Jesus passed over from life, through death, to new life. And we have the chance at the Easter Vigil to renew our baptismal promises which acknowledged our passing over, through the water of baptism to God's life in us.

— What "pass-over" do the first verses of this reading refer to?
— "Snuffed out, put out like a wick". How does this picture emphasise God's mighty power?
— "I am doing a new deed" says God. How do the next verses show the care God had for his people and the wonderful, nearly impossible, things he was prepared to do for them?

Second Reading

Read this carefully together. Notice how St Paul says, "All I want is to know Christ and the power of his resurrection and to share his sufferings by reproducing the pattern of his death".

— We could think for a minute if our Lent resolutions are helping us to know Jesus Christ better.

Opening prayer of the Mass

Father,
help us to be like Christ your Son,
who loved the world and died for our salvation.
Inspire us by his love
and guide us by his example.

Gospel Reading

In the first reading, we saw that God was "doing a new deed". Here in the Gospel, Jesus was also "doing a new deed". He was showing care and love and understanding for a woman who was despised. The religious men would have nothing to do with her.

— What does the saying mean: "Those who live in glass houses shouldn't throw stones?"
— How does Jesus show his respect for her embarrassment?
— How does he show that he expects her to live differently in the future?

Passion Sunday

— see page 29

Easter Day

— see page 30

As God the Father's power awoke Christ from death so we were raised to walk in newness of life

2nd Sunday of Easter   **Cycle C**

THE POWER OF JESUS

Things you need
Your Easter candle and flowers.

Prepare your Bible
New Testament: Acts, ch. 5, vv. 12-16.
                           St John, ch. 20, vv. 19-31.

First Reading
One of the first signs of the power of the Risen Lord among his disciples
was the healing of the sick.

— How did the people show their trust in Peter?

— What do you think Peter felt about this power given to him?

— How do you think the apostles found time for prayer in the demands made on them?

Gospel Reading

See 2nd Sunday of Easter, Cycle B, page 100.

3rd Sunday of Easter   *Cycle C*

JESUS AT BREAKFAST TIME

Things you need

Your Easter candle and flowers. Pictures of a boat, the sea or lakeside, fish as available. If there is a Guide or Scout who can light a fire in the garden, so much the better. You could make dampers.

Prepare your Bible

New Testament: Acts, ch. 5, vv. 27-32, 40-41.
                St John, ch. 21, vv. 1-19.

First Reading

Take parts to read this.

— What enabled Peter and his friends, ordinary fishermen, to speak so powerfully that they "filled Jerusalem with their teaching?"

— Can you think of someone in your own day who must have said as Peter said, "Obedience to God comes before obedience to men?"

— What was the belief for which they were willing to risk their lives?

Gospel Reading

In the Gospel we go back to the time when Peter was not so sure of himself. It needed the power of the Holy Spirit to "take him over" completely.

— Read this episode in parts. (The leader should know what characters he needs.)

- Which disciple was the first to recognise Jesus?
- Who took action — almost without thinking — once he knew it was Jesus on the shore?
- Has your family ever built a fire on the seashore? Build up a picture together in words of the scene St John describes — sounds, smells, textures, etc.

- Notice how Jesus asks the disciples to contribute to the meal. He invites them to share with him.

  At the meal of the Eucharist which we share each Sunday, what are we invited to contribute before receiving the gift of Jesus himself?
- The questioning of Peter. This time Peter said "Yes" but he must have remembered the three times he said "No". When was that? Jesus trusted Peter with the care of his "flock", the Church. That care continues through the Holy Father, our Bishops, priests and deacons.

  Let us pray for them often.

4th Sunday of Easter   *Cycle C*

WE BELONG TO JESUS

Things you need

Your Easter candle. Write out the text: "We are his people, the sheep of his flock".

Prepare your Bible

New Testament: Acts, ch. 13, vv. 14, 43-52.
Apocalypse, ch. 7, vv. 9, 14-17.
St John, ch. 10, vv. 27-30.

First Reading

There are different ways of hearing the Word of God.

— v. 43. How had these Jews listened?

— v. 45. How did these Jews react?

— vv. 47, 48. How did the pagans listen?

Is it possible to listen but not to hear the message? Can this sometimes happen to us at Mass?

In the prayer to the Holy Spirit we say: "O God who dost instruct the hearts of thy faithful by the light of the Holy Spirit, grant that by the gifts of the same Spirit we may be truly wise".

Second Reading

In the Mass we address Jesus as "The Lamb of God who takes away the sins of the world".

St John's vision of heaven is full of consolation for those who have "washed their robes white in the blood of the Lamb".

— Remind yourselves of the words of consecration at Mass.

— vv. 16, 17. Because a shepherd was the best example of someone who cares, Jesus (and his disciples after him) chose this image for himself. In these two verses, how does the description of heaven "come through" the care of the shepherd?

Gospel Reading

In the Lord's Prayer, we say "Our Father". Jesus says at the end of this reading, "The Father and I are one". If we say, "Our Father", we know that we belong to Jesus. "The sheep that belong to me" listen to Jesus and follow him. Jesus says: "I know them . . . I give them eternal life; they will never be lost".

— Let us think for a minute of what this means:

I belong to Jesus,
Do I listen to him and follow him?
Jesus knows me. He gives me eternal life.

Say together: We are his people, the sheep of his flock.

You might make up a verse about all this to the tune of "Thank you", e.g., Thank you for being our good shepherd,
Thank you for all your loving care . . .

ENTERING THE KINGDOM

Things you need
Your Easter candle. A dictionary.

Prepare your Bible
New Testament:
    Acts, ch. 14, vv. 21-27.
    Apocalypse, ch. 21, vv. 1-5.
    St John, ch. 13, vv. 31-35.

First Reading
We can see how much travelling the first apostles had to do in their work for Christ and his kingdom. How would they have travelled?
    v. 22. What kind of hardships might Paul and Barnabas be facing? And what kind of hardships faced new converts to Christianity? Do Christians these days have to suffer for their faith in the Risen Christ?

Second Reading
This week we hear St John's comparison of heaven to a beautiful bride.
    Read slowly the words coming from the voice from the throne. How do we know from this that heaven will be a happy place?
    v. 5. Think of some examples we have experienced of God making things new, e.g., the seasons, the seashore, forgiveness, surgery . . .

Prayer
We could use the response to the psalm as a prayer of thanksgiving for all the things we have just spoken about. "I will bless your name for ever, O God my King".

Gospel Reading
These words form part of the last talk Jesus had with his disciples before his death. Judas had gone to carry out his plans of betrayal and yet Jesus could say: "Now has the Son of Man been glorified . . .'

— Look up the word "Glory" in your dictionary. What do you mean when you say, "Glory be to the Father . . ." or "Glory to God in the highest . . ."?
— What is the new commandment?
— How does Jesus want people to know that we are Christians?
— Is there anything that we ought to decide to do in our family, at church, at school, at work so that we give a better and more obvious sign that we are friends of Jesus?

6th Sunday of Easter   *Cycle C*

THE PEACE OF THE KINGDOM

Things you need
Your Easter candle.

Prepare your Bible
New Testament: Acts, ch. 15, vv. 1, 2, 22-29.
                       Apocalypse, ch. 21, vv. 10-14, 22-23.
                       St John, ch. 14, vv. 23-29.

First Reading
Disagreement and argument! Life was not easy for the first Christians as they tried to bring the message of love and freedom to the pagans. They had, however, as we have today, the possibility of consulting the authorities in the Church. St Peter and some other apostles must have been in Jerusalem and it was they who wrote the letter in vv. 22-29.
    Who made the decision? See v. 28. What do you think this means?

Second Reading
This is another part of St John's vision — he seems to try every way he can think of, to tell us of the beauty of God and of heaven.
    vv. 22, 23. Re-read these two verses.
    What words or phrases do you like best?
    Do these verses speak to you of happiness or of peace or of security or of beauty? Is this a description of heaven that you like?

Gospel Reading

What reference to the Ascension of Jesus can you find? Look up the word "advocate" in your dictionary. Why do you think Jesus used it to talk about the Holy Spirit?

What will the Holy Spirit teach the disciples?

Look up the word "bequeath" in your dictionary. What gift is Jesus giving to his disciples?

— "Do not let your hearts be troubled or afraid". These words of Jesus were spoken to the apostles before his death. Perhaps they sensed that something terrible was going to happen to their leader. Would it be easy for them to be unafraid?

It is different for us. We know that the resurrection followed and that Jesus is alive now with us for ever. Let us ask for these words to penetrate our hearts. (Read them again slowly and leave a pause for silent prayer.)

Final prayer

Almighty and ever-living Lord,
you restored us to life
by raising Christ from death.
Strengthen us by this Easter sacrament.

7th Sunday of Easter   *Cycle C*

COME!

Things you need

Your Easter candle.

Prepare your Bible

New Testament: Acts, ch. 7, vv. 55-60.
                     Apocalypse, ch. 22, vv. 12-14, 16, 17, 20.
                     St John, ch. 17, vv. 20-26.

First Reading

Stephen was the first martyr — he gave his life for his faith in the resurrection of his master, Jesus. God showed him heaven before he died.

— What words did he use to give his life to God?

— What did he say which echoed the words of Jesus when he was being crucified?

— "He fell asleep". Do you like this way of describing the death of someone?

Second Reading

In John's vision today we hear the invitation to everyone to come to heaven. We were made by God to love him and to serve in this world and *to be happy with him for ever in the next.*

— It is Jesus who shows us the way to heaven and he says: "I shall indeed be with you".

Opening prayer

Let us pray that we may recognise the presence of Christ in our midst. (Pause.)

Father,
help us to keep in mind that Christ our Saviour
lives with you in glory,
and promised to remain with us until the end of time.

Gospel Reading

If these words are some of the last that Jesus spoke, they must be very important.

— Who is Jesus referring to in v. 20?

— What phrase recurs in vv. 21-23?

When do you feel most united as a family?

What other groups you belong to, give you a feeling of unity?

What kind of things unite people, even if only temporarily?

Would you say that unity amongst people lasts longest where there is love?

— v. 26. Jesus says he will "continue to make God's name known". How does this happen? Why is the Holy Spirit essential?

Conclusion

Can we think of some way in our family to ask for the Holy Spirit to enter our hearts afresh this Pentecost?

Pentecost — see page 39

Trinity Sunday — see page 40

2nd Sunday of the Year   ***Cycle C***

JESUS BRINGS HAPPINESS

Things you need

A picture or a photo of a wedding. Make a drawing of six water pots or have six jam jars ready in a row.

Prepare your Bible

Old Testament: Isaiah, ch. 62, vv. 1-5.
New Testament: St John, ch. 2, vv. 1-12.

First Reading

Read these few verses which form part of a poem promising hope and joy for the ruined Jerusalem. What references to rejoicing can you find?

How do people rejoice at a wedding?

Gospel Reading

St John's Gospel is not like the "synoptic" Gospels, Matthew, Mark and Luke, written as eye-witness accounts. (Synoptic comes from a Greek word. Syn — with, optic — eyes). John decided to choose a small number of events in the life of Jesus and to interpret them in order to bring out their deeper significance. He never used the word "sacrament" in his Gospel but the word he used a great deal was "sign". He chose seven "signs" or events in the life of Jesus in order to make clear two things:

1. To bring those who are not yet believers to accept Jesus as the Messiah, the Son of God.

173

2. To help Christians realise that they do not need to envy those who saw Jesus in bodily form, for Jesus lives on in the sacraments, in the worship of the Church, and in us all.

Read the passage. Write on your drawings the amount of liquid the water jars could hold or fill your jam jars with water as you read.

— What can you tell about a Jewish wedding feast from this account?
— Why do you think Mary noticed the shortage of wine?
— "He let his glory be seen". What does this mean? What effect did it have on the disciples?
— Jesus showed his glory by using ordinary people and things. If we have eyes to see and ears to hear, we too can see his glory
        — in the world around us
        — in people we meet.

Can you think of some examples?

Prayer
Say the "Glory be" together.

3rd Sunday of the Year   *Cycle C*

THE WORD OF GOD

Things you need
Make a special effort to show that you respect your Bible — put it on a cushion or a cloth, have a candle ready to light. Perhaps put a vase of flowers near it. Are your bookmarks still in good condition? Copy the words of Isaiah quoted in the Gospel on to a piece of paper and roll it up to make a scroll. Tie it round with a piece of ribbon or tape.

Prepare your Bible
Old Testament: Nehemiah, ch. 8, vv. 2-6, 8-10.
New Testament: St Luke, ch. 1, vv. 1-4; ch. 4, vv. 14-21.

First Reading
You could act this reading if the member of your family preparing it would tell you what to do in advance.

— How can you tell that the Book of the Law was so important to the people? Notice what the people and Ezra did.

Compare the people listening to Ezra to our listening to the Word of God at Mass.
> — where the reader stands to read
> — how the people listen
> — how the people show respect for the message
> — how the message is explained

— If you have Bibles other than the one you are using, for example, at school, are they well cared for? Do they need a new cover? Do we hold them carefully?

Gospel Reading

Read the passage with one person taking the part of Jesus using the scroll you have made.

The Jews used to invite well-known guests to read from the Scriptures and then to preach during their service in the synagogue on the Sabbath day. Jesus was beginning to be well-known and, as Nazareth was his home town, the people wanted to hear what he had to say.

— Did Jesus choose the passage to read or was it chosen for him?
— Why would these verses have caught the attention of the congregation?
— "He sat down . . . and began to speak to them". What were the first words of his sermon? What would have been their effect on his listeners?

A practical point

It is a privilege to proclaim the Word of God. Good readers are needed in our parishes to read at Mass. Has anyone in your family volunteered to do so?

TRUTH MUST BE SPOKEN

Prepare your Bible

Old Testament: Jeremiah, ch. 1, vv. 4, 5, 17-19.
New Testament: St Luke, ch. 4, vv. 21-30.

Other preparation

If the leader is not sure of the Old Testament stories quoted by Jesus in the Gospel, look up 1 Kings, ch. 17, vv. 7-16 and 2 Kings, ch. 5, vv. 1-5, 9-14.

First Reading

Jeremiah was called by God to deliver unpleasant messages to his people, but he also assured them of God's continual love and care.

Read the passage together:

— How can we tell that God loved his people?

— What pictures does God use to describe how he will support and bring victory to his people?

— If Jeremiah was writing today, what metals and materials would he have mentioned as being strong enough to symbolise God's strengthening of his people in danger?

Gospel Reading

You notice that this week's reading continues from last Sunday. As the congregation listened to Jesus, their reactions to his words gradually changed.

— What was their first reaction? — first half of v. 22.

— Their second reaction? — end of v. 22.

— The reaction in v. 28?

— Can you guess how they felt after the event in v. 30?
Ask your leader to remind you of the stories Jesus quoted. Neither the widow of Zarephtha nor the leper Naaman were Jews. Why did the mention of these two people make the worshippers in the synagogue so angry?

— By mentioning these two incidents where God took such wonderful care of non-Jews, what was Jesus trying to tell them?

176

Prayer

We could think if there are people or groups of people who we are inclined to ignore or despise or to keep outside our friendship and goodwill. The opening prayer of the Mass leads us to pray for a greater love of God and of our fellow-men.

Lord our God,
help us to love you with all our hearts
and to love all men as you love them.
Amen.

5th Sunday of the Year   *Cycle C*

GOD'S MESSENGERS

Things you need

Write on two separate pieces of paper: "Here I am, send me" and "Don't be afraid".

Prepare your Bible

Old Testament: Isaiah, ch. 6, vv. 1-8.
New Testament: St Luke, ch. 5, vv. 1-11.

First Reading

This vision of Isaiah seems to have taken place in the Temple at Jerusalem. How does the song of the angels compare with "Holy, holy, holy" we say or sing at Mass? The priest invites us to join our voices with . . . whom?

Isaiah was aware that he was in the presence of God Almighty and this made him acknowledge his unworthiness. What do we say at Mass before receiving Our Lord in Holy Communion, which expresses the same kind of knowledge of ourselves?

But God wanted Isaiah to be his messenger. In his vision, one of the angels seemed to purify his lips. Then he heard the call of God — and you have written Isaiah's reply.

177

L

Gospel Reading

Read about the wonderful trust of Peter, the fisherman, in Jesus. If no fish had been caught during the night then it was highly unlikely that they would be near the surface in broad daylight, 'but if you say so . . .'

— Why did Peter say: "Leave me, Lord. I am a sinful man"?

— You have written down part of the reply Jesus made. When God asks us to do something for him, to be his messenger, we have no need to be afraid.

Prayer

Put your two phrases where everyone can see them.

Look forward to the week to come — is any one of you afraid of some event? Let's pray that we shall respond to God's call this week and remember the words of Jesus: "Don't be afraid".

Father,
watch over your family
and keep us safe in your care,
for all our hope is in you.
Amen.

6th Sunday of the Year   *Cycle C*

REAL HAPPINESS

Things you need

Draw a dried up bush in the desert and a tree beside a stream so that you can see its roots reaching the water. Write the word HAPPY and decorate it.

Prepare your Bible

Old Testament: Jeremiah, ch. 17, vv. 5-8.
New Testament: St Luke, ch. 17, vv. 20-26.

First Reading

Do you remember the long hot summer of 1976? Did your family suffer from the drought that year?

Remind the younger members of the ways we had to save water.

As you read the passage from Jeremiah, have your two pictures ready. Jeremiah wants us to understand that we must place all our trust in God's love and care. Our trust must be like the roots of the tree you have drawn. Even when troubles come, deep in our hearts we must trust God, who will never fail us.

Can you think of some troubles in our lives which disturb the surface? Have you read stories of people in concentration camps or in prison who kept their faith in God?

Response to the Psalm

"Happy the man who has placed his trust in the Lord".

You might like to write this response on your picture for the youngest member to take to Mass.

Gospel Reading

Notice how people had to come from far away to hear Jesus — rather like a rally these days, or a mission.

— When someone speaks to you, looking you straight in the eyes, you know you must listen carefully.

— "Happy are you who are poor" — you are free to belong to God. What can keep us selfish and concerned about ourselves and our welfare?

— "Happy are you who are hungry now" — do we know what joy there is on Family Fast Day in helping those who need food to survive?

— "Happy are you who weep now" — Sharing other people's sadness, understanding their unhappiness sometimes makes us sad ourselves, but we are doing what Jesus would do and this brings us joy.

Prayer

It is sad, dear Lord, if we won't stop to help others. They are our brothers. May everything we do be guided by your law of love.

BE COMPASSIONATE

Things you need

Something like a spear and a pitcher of water. Write out: "The Lord is compassion and love".

Prepare your Bible

Old Testament: 1 Samuel, ch. 26, vv. 2, 7-9, 12-13, 22-23.
New Testament: St Luke, ch. 6, vv. 27-38.

First Reading

The reading at Mass will not be the whole of the chapter but your family could read and act this episode in David's life. David had to escape from Saul who wanted to kill him. We see how loyal David was to his King because he believed him to be God's choice for the people.

Read verse 12 quietly together if you can — God has ways of taking care of those he loves.

Response to the Psalm

"The Lord is compassion and love". How did David show this compassion? How does the Lord show compassion and love through our parents, doctors, probation officers, priests, friends, etc.?

Gospel Reading

Jesus means us to take these words seriously if we intend to be his followers. Read the passage straight through, though Jesus may not have said all these things at the same time to his disciples. Probably St Luke has grouped together the way Jesus told his disciples to act on many different occasions.

But these words are for us. Let us try to see how they apply to us.
— Do good to those who hate you. How?
— Pray for those who treat you badly. Who should we pray for *now*? "Forgive us our trespasses as we forgive . . . who have trespassed against us".
— To the man who slaps you on one cheek . . . This may be a slap in the form of words. How difficult it is not to answer back!

— Do not judge. Only God sees into my heart and into your heart to know why we do things that seem strange or annoying or hurtful to others.

Prayer

Let us pray that God will make us more like Christ, his Son.
Father,
keep before us the wisdom and love
you have revealed in your Son.
Help us to be like him
in word and deed,
for he lives and reigns with you and the Holy Spirit,
one God, for ever and ever. Amen.

8th Sunday of the Year   *Cycle C*

THE REAL 'ME'

Things you need

If you have young children in your family, you may need to show them a sieve (garden or kitchen) and be ready to describe a kiln.

Prepare your Bible

Old Testament: Ecclesiasticus, ch. 27, vv. 4-7.
New Testament: St Luke, ch. 6, vv. 39-45.

First Reading

These verses help us to consider the things we say and the way we say them. Once words have been spoken they cannot be recaptured and they show to other people the person we really are.

Think together about each picture painted for us in this reading:
— Are we inclined to remember the unpleasant things people say and forget the good things?
— How does a kiln test the quality of a pot?
— Would you say that words are the fruit of our thoughts?

— A poet has the gift of expressing himself in words. Sometimes a song or hymn or a psalm can say more than straightforward speech. Can you think of an example?

Responsorial Psalm

Here is the first verse of the psalm for Sunday.

> It is good to give thanks to the Lord
> to make music to your name, O Most High,
> to proclaim your love in the morning
> and your truth in the watches of the night.

Gospel Reading

— vv. 39-42. Do you think that Jesus made his listeners smile at these examples, even though he was giving them a very serious lesson? Try to imagine the two men with the splinter and the plank!

— vv. 41-45. These words of Jesus echo the examples in the first reading.

— We must be honest and straightforward, not playing a part but being the person God made us to be.

The Confiteor

At the beginning of every Mass, we are invited to think about ourselves, to consider the ways in which we have not been the person God made us to be, and to ask for his forgiveness.

> I confess . . .
> that I have sinned through my own fault,
> in my thoughts and in my words,
> in what I have done and in what I have failed to do.

— Let us pause for a moment now to think about this and then say the "I Confess" together.

GOD IS FOR ALL PEOPLE

Things you need

A lighted candle. Place round your candle pictures of as many different races of people that you can find.

Prepare your Bible

Old Testament: 1 Kings, ch. 8, vv. 41-43.
New Testament: St Luke, ch. 7, vv. 1-10.

Prayer

Look at the pictures your leader has found. See how the light of the candle is spread over them all. You remember that Jesus said, "I am the light of the world". Think of any friends you have who are not of the same nationality as you.

Here is the Responsorial Psalm for Sunday:

O praise the Lord, all you nations,
acclaim him all you peoples!
Strong is his love for us;
he is faithful for ever.

First Reading

Many Jews believed that they, as the Chosen People, were set apart. This, in a way, was true, for from their race Jesus, the Saviour, was to be born. Read how Solomon, who had prayed for wisdom, longs for God to be worshipped by all men.

Gospel Reading

A centurion was a Roman soldier in charge of one hundred men.

— How can we tell that he was friendly towards the Jews?

— How can we tell that these Jewish elders were sympathetic towards Jesus and trusted him?

— Why did the centurion send a message to save Jesus the trouble of coming to his house?

— v. 7. We say words like this just before we receive Holy Communion. What words do we say?

— Why was Jesus so overcome at the man's attitude?

Conclusion

Sit quietly round your lighted candle. Think of the centurion sending to Jesus for help.

Let us ask for any special help we need.

Say slowly together the prayer before Holy Communion.

Lord, I am not worthy to receive you,
but only say the word and I shall be healed.

10th Sunday of the Year   *Cycle C*

SORROW TURNED INTO JOY

Prepare your Bible

Old Testament: 1 Kings, ch. 17, vv. 17-24.
New Testament: St Luke, ch. 7, vv. 11-17.

Theme song from the Psalm

For me you have changed my mourning into dancing;
O Lord my God, I will thank you for ever.

(Could the family leader illustrate this with colour?)

First Reading

Just before this incident, Elijah had saved the woman and her son from starvation during a very severe famine. She had been grateful to the prophet at that time but when her son became ill, she viewed the presence of Elijah in a different light.

— How did she feel about him then?

— Where did he carry the sick boy?

— How did he pray?

— What did he do as well as pray? Does this remind you of a method of resuscitation used today?

— Would the "theme song" from the psalm be a suitable prayer for the woman?

Gospel Reading

Many of the towns in Israel were walled towns to afford protection. The gates leading in and out of the town would have to be guarded in cases of emergency.

Burial grounds were always outside the towns as a health precaution. There was very little delay between death and burial in a country that was often very hot.

— How can we tell that Nain was a walled town?
— What made this boy's death particularly sad for his mother?
— What did Jesus do to restore him to his mother?
— Would the "theme song" from the psalm be a suitable prayer for this woman?
— What effect did this miracle have on all who were attending the funeral?

To think and pray about

There are many events in our lives when we pass from sadness to joy. Here are a few suggestions. Can you add to them?

— losing and finding something precious
— breaking an arm and then, later, coming out of plaster
— hurting someone badly and then making it up.

God is always with us, ready to help and heal, to forgive and to comfort. Let us think of this for a moment and then say together the "theme song".

11th Sunday of the Year   *Cycle C*

FORGIVENESS

Prepare your Bible

Old Testament: 2 Samuel, ch. 12, vv. 7-10, 13.
New Testament: St Luke, ch. 7, v. 36, ch. 8, v. 3.

First Reading

This passage follows the wonderful story Nathan told in order to help King David recognise his sin and repent. The leader should read chapter 11 and the beginning of chapter 12 so that he can remind the family of the situation.

— Nathan made David remember all the things God had done for him. What were they?

— What punishment did David expect for his sin?

— "Forgive, Lord, the guilt of my sin". This is the response to the psalm. Listen carefully on Sunday to the psalm. How ready God is to forgive!

Gospel Reading

Jesus was the friend of sinners. They recognised this and were not afraid to approach him. No one is happy if they know they have something on their conscience. Jesus came to bring happiness. In many cases this is reached through forgiveness.

— Would it have taken courage for the woman to push her way into this rich household?

— Why was Simon annoyed with the incident?

— What story did Jesus tell to help Simon and the other guests understand the real meaning of the woman's action?

— "Go in peace". Is this phrase ever said to us after we have been forgiven?

— When we have had to apologise to one another, what sign do we sometimes give that all is forgiven?

Prayer

Let us ask for God's help that we may be forgiving people and that we may know how to ask for forgiveness.

Almighty God,
our hope and our strength,
without you we falter.
Help us to follow Christ
and to live according to your will.

GO IN PEACE !

THE SAVIOUR

Things you need
A crucifix in the centre of your family.

Prepare your Bible
Old Testament: Zechariah, ch. 12, vv. 10-11.
New Testament: St Luke, ch. 9, vv. 18-24.

First Reading
From our Christian viewpoint we can read into this passage the passion and death of Jesus. These verses contain God's promise to take care of his people.
— v. 10. What gift does God promise to his people?
— How does the rest of the verse make you think of Jesus?
— v. 11. This probably refers to some pagan celebration.

Gospel Reading
See the 24th Sunday of Cycle B, page 136.

COME, FOLLOW ME

Things you need
Arrange on the table where your family gathers, a display of things which are signs that you are followers of Jesus: e.g., a crucifix, a cross you wear, a confirmation certificate, etc.

Prepare your Bible
Old Testament: 1 Kings, ch. 19, vv. 16, 19-21.
New Testament: St Luke, ch. 9, vv. 51-62.

First Reading

Elijah was nearing the end of his life, but his work as God's spokesman had to go on.

— How did Elijah know to whom he had to pass his power and authority?

— Where did he find his successor?

— Throwing the cloak over Elisha symbolised Elijah's taking possession of him. How do we know that Elisha realised that he could not resist this call?

— What did Elisha do to show that he accepted God's call and was putting his old life behind him?

Gospel Reading

vv. 51-56. We have an example of how the Samaritans hated the Jews. The fact that Jesus and his disciples were on a pilgrimage to Jerusalem would make them even less ready to receive them as guests in their village.

— What did the disciples feel about this rejection?

— How did Jesus deal with the situation?

— vv. 57-62. How do these verses link up with our First Reading?

— How do the replies that Jesus gave to the three men who wanted to follow him, show that Christians must be prepared to be completely unselfish?

To consider

Each one of us has taken certain steps to follow Jesus. What signs of these steps have you prepared for the family to look at?

— Each time we meet Jesus Christ in the sacraments, we are taking a step with him. In the Eucharist we ask him to enter our lives and make us more like him,

— in the Sacrament of Reconciliation, we ask him to take away all that separates us from him and to fill us with his own Spirit.

— Many times each day we choose to act for him in love, joy, helpfulness, unselfishness. Our hand was "laid on the plough" at our baptism. Talk about this.

Prayer   Lord God,
through your sacraments
you give us the power of your grace.
May this eucharist
help us to serve you faithfully.

PEACE

Things you need

Make a little poster which says "PEACE" and fix it (at the beginning of the day) to the door of the room where your family is going to meet.

Prepare your Bible

Old Testament: Isaiah, ch. 66, vv. 10-14.
New Testament: St Luke, ch. 10, vv. 1-12, 17-20.

First Reading

Before you read the passage, ask each member of the family to describe the most peaceful spot they know. You may perhaps find that you have a common experience from your summer holidays. You might like to look at the photos you have taken.

— Now read Isaiah's description of peace and joy. He concentrates more on peace in a relationship. Ask your mother how important she found it to feed you in peace when you were a baby.

— God uses this picture to show how he takes care of us and comforts us. Do you think it is a good picture?

Gospel Reading

We read how Jesus did not prepare only the twelve apostles to be his missionaries, though they had special responsibility. He needed other people to prepare the way for him as well.

— Why did Jesus say he was sending them out "like lambs among wolves?"

— How can we tell that Jesus planned where each pair was to go?

— What message did they carry?

— What else did they do during their mission?

— When they came home, the disciples were jubilant at all they had been able to do with the power Jesus had given them. What did Jesus teach them was the real cause for rejoicing?

Greetings at Mass

At the beginning of Mass, the priest welcomes us with one of three greetings. Here is one of them:

"The grace and peace of God our Father and the Lord Jesus Christ be with you".

Just before we receive Holy Communion, the priest prays for peace:

Lord Jesus Christ, you said to your apostles:
I leave you peace, my peace I give you.
Look not on our sins, but on the faith of your Church,
and grant us the peace and unity of your kingdom
where you live for ever and ever.

Then we are invited to give each other a sign of peace:

"The peace of the Lord be with you always. — Let us offer each other a sign of peace."

Prayer

Let us prepare for this moment by thinking quietly if there is anyone with whom we are not at peace and asking for the help we need to restore it.

15th Sunday of the Year   *Cycle C*

WITHIN MY HEART

Things you need

Find a picture or an account of someone helping an unknown person in distress.

Prepare your Bible

Old Testament: Deuteronomy, ch. 30, vv. 10-14.
New Testament: St Luke, ch. 10, vv. 25-37.

First Reading

Let us pray for a moment that we may open our hearts to God's message for us.

— Read the passage slowly and say at the end, "This is the Word of the Lord". "Thanks be to God".

— This understanding of God's nearness was held by people who lived about 1,300 years before Christ was born. It is not difficult to love and serve God our Maker — no need to go to heaven itself or to cross the sea to find the way. Where is this Word of God?

— For us, baptised Christians, who know that St John called Jesus "the Word", how easy it should be to live close to God!

Prayer

> God our Father,
> your light of truth
> guides us to the way of Christ.
> Help us to follow the Word we find in our heart.

Gospel Reading

— Why did Jesus have to tell this story?

— You will remember that Samaritans disliked Jews (see 13th Sunday, page 188). How does this fact make the story very powerful?

— Who does Jesus mean us to understand by our "neighbour"?

— What do you think of the innkeeper's part in the incident?

To consider

Share the picture or account that you found in preparing this session. Can any member of the family suggest another example of a "Good Samaritan"? e.g., on the motorway, in the playground, in the supermarket, on the beach.

Theme of the two Readings

It is not difficult to love God. His Spirit is within our hearts to direct us. All creatures are signs of his presence for us to love and to serve.

— Say together: "You must love the Lord your God with all your heart, with all your soul, with all your strength and with all your mind, and your neighbour as yourself". Lord, please help us.

WELCOME!

Things you need

Prepare a card which says WELCOME and put it where your family are going to meet. Put a small vase of flowers beside it.

Prepare your Bible

Old Testament: Genesis, ch. 18, vv. 1-10.
New Testament: St Luke, ch. 10, vv. 38-42.

First Reading

When Abraham first saw the three men, he had no idea that this was the way God was choosing to appear to him. With the typical hospitality of Eastern people, he invited them to stay with him for a meal.

— What meal did he ask his wife Sarah to prepare?
— What other courtesy did he show them while they were waiting?
— According to the customs of the desert tribes, Sarah did not come out to meet her husband's guests. What great promise did she hear from inside the tent?

Gospel Reading

Jesus was always made welcome at Bethany by Lazarus and his two sisters. He must have known them well enough to be able to drop in for a meal. Mary and Martha were both delighted to see him but they showed their love in two different ways. How did each of them show their pleasure in welcoming Jesus?

— Jesus appreciated both sisters and was anxious that each one should be completely herself. A Jesuit retreat-giver said: "If there had been two Marys, there would have been no supper and if there had been two Marthas there would have been no peace to eat it!"

To consider

— When we have guests in our home, how do we make them welcome?
— When one of our family comes home late or tired or ill or in trouble, are we thoughtful and kind?

— Do we try to appreciate the ways in which we are different, instead of expecting that everyone will see things from our point of view?
— Is our home a place where Jesus himself would feel welcome?

Another text

I stand at the door and knock, says the Lord. If anyone hears my voice and opens the door, I will come in and sit down to supper with him, and he with me.

Come to my heart, Lord Jesus.

17th Sunday of the Year   *Cycle C*

HOW GOOD GOD IS!

Prepare your Bible

Old Testament: Genesis, ch. 18, vv. 20-32.
New Testament: St Luke, ch. 11, vv. 1-13.

First Reading

You will see that there are only a few verses between last Sunday's reading and this one. You might like to read them.

It seems that one of the three men that Abraham had entertained was God himself accompanied by two angels — all in the form of men. Thus God speaks and thinks as a man in this text according to the writer.

— Read the courageous way in which Abraham pleaded for God's mercy on sinful men.
— This narrative illustrates the age-old problem of the way good people sometimes suffer with and for the wicked. Jeremiah tells a story in which one good person was enough for God to save a whole people. In what very special way did this come true?

193

Gospel Reading

— vv. 1-4. The disciples must have observed Jesus at prayer many times and it made them wish to pray like him. Take these lines from St Luke and compare them with the Lord's prayer that we say.

— vv. 9-12. These verses concern "the prayer of petition" — the kind of prayer where we ask God for what we need.

— How does the friend obtain the bread he needs in the end? So we must persevere in asking God.

— Just as a father gives his child the best thing for him and not necessarily what the child has asked for, so God answers our prayers.

If a very small child said, "Give me, give me", pointing to a stone or a snake or a scorpion, what would his father do?

— v. 13. What great gift will the Father always give if we ask for it?

To discuss

Can you look back over a few years or over many years and see how God's hand has guided your life by an event or a person which at the time you resented or did not understand?

Part of the Psalm

>"Your hand will do all things for me.
>Your love, O Lord, is eternal".

Let us tell God quietly that we trust him.

18th Sunday of the Year   *Cycle C*

CHRIST IS EVERYTHING!

Prepare your Bible

New Testament: Colossians, ch. 3, vv. 1-5, 9-11.
                St Luke, ch. 12, vv. 13-21.

Second Reading (of the Mass)

St Paul is helping us to see that we must not be preoccupied with trivial things — with things that centre on ourselves and our own pleasure.

We have a great future promised to us, not visible at the moment — vv. 3, 4.

— vv. 9, 10. Perhaps this refers to the baptism of the early Christians who took off their clothes before they were immersed in the water and then put on their baptismal garment. A new life had begun! What white garment were you given during your baptism?

The priest said to you, "X, you have become a new creation, and have clothed yourself in Christ. See in this white garment the outward sign of your Christian dignity".

vv. 10, 11. This new life given us in baptism is meant to grow and progress so that we become more like God. We could think of contrasting groups of people today, e.g., black and white, Catholics and Protestants, workers and management, etc., which could not exist in opposition if the image of God in each one was allowed to grow and to shine through.

Gospel Reading

Jesus wants us all to know that the most precious things in life are not material things which we can collect and on which we think we can rely for comfort and security.

— Why do you think the man was anxious to have his share of the inheritance at once?

— In this parable, the rich man thought he was making a nice little nest for himself for the rest of his life. What had he forgotten?

— Could we ever act like this man without realising it? e.g., accepting a Sunday job to earn money which might prevent us going to Mass? Working overtime for the same reason? Working or playing too late at night to be able to pray?

Prayer after Communion

Lord,
you give us the strength of new life
by the gift of the eucharist.
Protect us with your love
and prepare us for eternal redemption.

GOD CHOOSES HIS MOMENT

Prepare your Bible

Old Testament: Wisdom, ch. 18, vv. 6-9.
New Testament: St Luke, ch. 12, vv. 32-48.

First Reading

These verses are amongst those referring
back to the great night when God freed
his people from the Egyptians by allowing
them to cross the Reed Sea (now called
the Red Sea) and escape.

— v. 6. The children of Israel had accepted God's promise. Now they
could see that they could trust him.

— v. 7. What does this mean?

— v. 9. The Passover meal was a sacrifice and it was held secretly
in the people's own homes before they left Egypt. They sang
psalms and hymns during the meal. These would continue to be
sung by future generations wherever the Passover was celebated.

Response to the Psalm

"Happy are the people the Lord has chosen as his own".

The Jews knew they were God's Chosen People. Can we say this
response with the same conviction about ourselves?

Gospel Reading

Jesus continues the teaching we read last Sunday, about being sure
we are concerned with our love of God instead of worrying too much
over earthly possessions. Have you ever had a purse that wore out,
perhaps the zip broke? Or have you lost money by having a hole in your
pocket? The good and kind things we do because we love God, can
never be lost.

— vv. 35-48. Imagine the household of servants waiting for the arrival
of the master — someone posted at the window all the time. What
do you think of v. 38? Remember that a parable has a hidden meaning. v. 40 gives the clue. What does it mean?

— There are two kinds of servants. How would you describe the character of each?

To consider

The end of v. 48. We have been given talents and gifts and strengths. When God created us, he entrusted us with these wonderful treasures. When we were baptised, he entrusted us with the gift of faith. Our parents and godparents were asked to nourish these gifts for us until we could be responsible for them ourselves.

Let us think for a moment about ourselves and the gifts we have within us.

Let us thank God for these gifts.

Let us ask that, through these gifts, we may grow in the knowledge and love of God.

20th Sunday of the Year   *Cycle C*

TRIALS AND VICTORY

Prepare your Bible

Old Testament: Jeremiah, ch. 38, vv. 4-6, 8-10.
New Testament: St Luke, ch. 12, vv. 49-53.

First Reading

Jeremiah was born 450 years before Christ. He lived through very difficult times. God used him to warn the Jews of tragedy, of war and of suffering but they would not listen to him. At the time of our story this week, Jeremiah was a captive in Jerusalem. First he was put in an underground cell but later he was kept where he could receive visitors. He was then accused of undermining the courage of the soldiers who were guarding Jerusalem from attack.

— Where did they put Jeremiah as further punishment?
— Do you think they proposed to feed him?
— Who interceded for him with the king?
— We are told that the men let down rags for Jeremiah to fix under his arms to prevent the rope rubbing him as he was hauled up!

Response to Psalm   "Lord, come to my aid".

This could have been Jeremiah's prayer while he was down the well. Listen carefully to the verses of the psalm on Sunday. They could have been exactly the kind of prayer Jeremiah would have said to God.

Gospel Reading

vv. 49, 50. Jesus is referring to his crucifixion. He died to save us from sin and so the fire to which he is referring is a fire that cleanses and purifies. From the moment of his death he won victory over sin and he wants us all to be purified.

— vv. 51-53. To accept the saving power of Jesus demands a decision. Each one of us has to make this decision for himself, over and over again.

— When could this decision to live for Jesus bring division into our lives? Christ must come first.

Prayer

> God our Father,
> may we love you in all things and above all things
> and reach the joy you have prepared for us
> beyond all our imaginings.

21st Sunday of the Year   *Cycle C*

LET THEM ALL COME

Things you need

Make a centre piece on your table of a globe or map of the world, a crucifix and a lighted candle.

Prepare your Bible

Old Testament: Isaiah, ch. 66, vv. 18-21.
New Testament: St Luke, ch. 13, vv. 22-30.

First Reading

We often read of God's desire to bring all people to himself. In this list of places, Isaiah has chosen the limits of his known world, probably from Spain to the Black Sea, with an indication of still more faraway places.

— When God calls all these people together, what are they to see?

— How does Isaiah indicate the number and variety of people who will come?

— Where does he consider to be the centre of God's world?

Gospel Reading

We see that hundreds of years later, Jesus is making his way to this same centre of the Jewish world. But Jesus is concerned with the Kingdom of God which needs no city walls and buildings.

— Jesus is not meaning to be selective when he implies that it is difficult to enter this kingdom. You remember last week how we saw that it needs a definite decision to serve Christ. When he calls, we must answer. We cannot take it for granted that if we have answered once, that will last us all our life. We have to be loving and serving God always.

— Some of the Jews were inclined to think that because they were Jews and chosen by God, they had no more efforts to make. Which verse seems to be directed at them?

— v. 29. Notice how this links up with the reading from Isaiah.

— v. 30. Jesus was full of surprises. He often chose the most unlikely people to help him and to be his friends. Can you think of any?

Prayer

Let us think for a moment if there are any people we are inclined to ignore or to despise or to neglect because we feel we are better than they are in some way.

For the times we have hurt others by ignoring them — Lord have mercy.

For the times we have not welcomed people in a friendly way — Christ have mercy.

For the times we have forgotten that you love everyone — Lord have mercy.

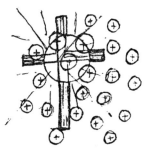

Thy kingdom come. Thy will be done on earth as it is in heaven.

GENTLENESS AND HUMILITY

Prepare your Bible

Old Testament: Ecclesiasticus, ch. 3, vv. 17-20, 28-29.
New Testament: St Luke, ch. 14, vv. 1, 7-14.

First Reading

— Sometimes we can worry because we are unable to be as generous as we would like with things that cost money. What is more important than that?

— Can you think of a great man or woman, a well-known and famous person who strikes you as "behaving humbly?"

— "He accepts the homage of the humble". With what words do we begin the Preface of the Mass? With whom do we, little creatures made by God, join our voices to tell God that he is great and holy?

Gospel Reading

vv. 1, 7-11. When you have read these verses, try to make up a modern parable with the same meaning, e.g., at a dinner party, choosing a room at a conference house, at a concert.

vv. 12-14. Jesus did not mean this to be taken literally. It is good to invite our relations and friends for a meal. It is a way to celebrate our friendship and to deepen it. It is because a meal is a sign of friendship, that Jesus chose to give himself to us in the context of a sacrificial meal.

It was the motive behind the invitation that Jesus meant.

Talk about this for a few moments.

Prayer

Here is a prayer of St Ignatius of Loyola, the founder of the Jesuits (the Society of Jesus). We celebrate his feast on July 31st.

Teach us, good Lord, to be generous,
to serve you as you deserve,
To give and not to count the cost,
to fight, and not to heed the wounds,
to toil, and not to seek for rest,
to labour, and *not to ask for any reward save that of
knowing that we do your will.*

23rd Sunday of the Year   *Cycle C*

THE POWER OF GOD'S WISDOM

Things you need

During the week, look out for reports on television or in the papers
of research and discoveries.

Prepare your Bible

Old Testament: Wisdom, ch. 9, vv. 13-18.
New Testament: St Luke, ch. 14, vv. 25-33.

First Reading

Talk for a few moments about the discoveries you have heard of during
this week — in medicine, in archeology, in space travel, etc.

Read the passage from the Book of Wisdom and see how it describes
man's struggle to conquer the mysteries of the world.

— How does the writer show that it is God who gives all skill and
   intelligence?

— In the Creed we say: We believe in one God, the Father, the
   Almighty, maker of heaven and earth, of all that is, seen and
   unseen.

   We are aware of God's creation through the senses he has given
   us. Use these questions to help you realise the wonder of God:

   Sight — What is the most beautiful and greatest thing you have
              seen? The most beautiful and smallest thing?

   Smell — What is the loveliest smell?

   Taste — What is the sweetest and most savoury taste?

N

Touch — The most encouraging, soothing, cold things?

Hearing — The most exciting, beautiful, peaceful sounds?

WE BELIEVE IN GOD THE MAKER OF ALL THAT IS.

Gospel Reading

In these verses Jesus tells us how serious a thing it is to decide to follow him. v. 26. Hate here means detachment. We follow Jesus according to the way he calls us; some follow him as married people, some as unmarried; some as priests and brothers, some as nuns. Deciding on our vocation needs prayer and consideration and advice.

— Read the two examples Jesus gives of building a tower and of going to war.

— Now look back to Wisdom, ch. 9, v. 17. It is the Holy Spirit to whom we turn for guidance all our life to be sure we are following Christ in the way he wishes.

Prayer from the Psalm

Let the favour of the Lord be upon us:
give success to the work of our hands.

24th Sunday of the Year   *Cycle C*

GOD'S LOVING FORGIVENESS

Prepare your Bible

Old Testament: Exodus, ch. 32, vv. 7-11, 13-14.

New Testament: St Luke, ch. 15, vv. 1-32.

First Reading

Moses was the leader of God's chosen people and he felt responsible for them and often prayed for them. "In prayer, man turns to God and listens for his Word". Moses spent many days alone in the mountains with God, learning through prayer what he had to teach his people.

— In our reading we are told that the people became tired of waiting for Moses to return with news of their God. What did they do in his absence?

202

— The writer puts human words and reactions into God's mouth. How did Moses plead with God?
— We often ask God to forgive us. Sometimes we ask for forgiveness for other people — those who ill-treat children, those who make bombs to injure others, those who attack old people, etc.
— Here is a prayer from the psalm:

> Have mercy on me, God, in your kindness,
> In your compassion blot out my offence.
> O wash me more and more from my guilt
> and cleanse me from my sin.

Gospel Reading

We have three "lost and found" stories. Find out from vv. 1-3, why Jesus told these parables.

— Read the story of the lost sheep and the lost coin.
If Jesus was telling these parables today, what examples might he have chosen? e.g., a lost wedding ring? a lost piece of jigsaw puzzle? a lost stamp for a collection? . . .
— The lost son. Why do you think he left home?
— The father. Could he have prevented his son going away?
— The brother. Why was he jealous of his young brother?
— When the runaway boy met his father, did he get to the end of the speech he had prepared?
— The ring was a sign of rank and the sandals a sign of being a son of the family. Have you heard the saying, "to kill the fatted calf".
— What ways of celebrating would you find the same today in a home-coming party?
— Why is this a good parable to read while preparing for the Sacra- of Reconciliation?

Prayer

Almighty God,
our creator and guide,
may we serve you with all our heart
and know your forgiveness in our lives.

BE FAIR AND JUST

Things you need

A picture from a CAFOD appeal or any other Third World literature which you may find in the newspaper.

If there are young children in the family, a pair of scales to explain the first reading.

Prepare your Bible

Old Testament: Amos, ch. 8, vv. 4-7.
New Testament: St Luke, ch. 16, vv. 10-13.

First Reading

During the time of the New Moon, like the Sabbath, no work was allowed. The people referred to seem to have only one idea in life — to make money.

— How did they cheat their customers?

— What kind of people suffered the most?

— How can we tell that the vendors squeezed every penny from the sale of their wheat?

— In the world today, there are poor and rich countries. How are we encouraged to work for justice for the poorer nations?

— God is the Father of all men. How did Amos warn the oppressors that their deeds were not unnoticed by God?

Gospel Reading

The Gospel you hear on Sunday may be longer than the verses we have noted — vv. 1-13 — but because even scholars find the first part very difficult, we are not attempting to study it.

— Think of various ways in which parents gradually help their children to take responsibility, e.g., going out to play, going shopping, having a key to the house, etc.

— God has given us different kinds of possessions. There are things we can touch and hold, buy and sell.

There are wonderful gifts within us such as memory, our talents and skills, our ability to make decisions, gifts of a generous and loving heart, patience, wisdom, joy . . . These are the greatest gifts. God gradually trusts us as we grow and develop in love and service of him. How can we show him that we value these gifts and want to use them for his glory?

— v. 13. All that God gives us is good. How can we be sure that we put God first in our lives, because we "cannot be the slave both of God and of money?"

Prayer

Let us thank God quietly for all he has given us and ask ourselves if we share generously with those people who are in need.

> "Give us this day our daily bread, God our Father, and help us to do what we can for the hungry who are our brothers".

26th Sunday of the Year   *Cycle C*

LUXURIOUS LIVING
IS NOT TRUE LIFE

Prepare your Bible

Old Testament: Amos, ch. 6, vv. 1, 4-7.
New Testament: St Luke, ch. 16, vv. 19-31.

First Reading

Amos lived about 750 BC at a time when there was a great contrast between rich and poor. The rich people had stone houses which were often panelled with wood and ivory inlay. The poor lived in great distress which was made worse by the way the rich people exploited them and treated them unjustly.

— Read the description of some of the luxuries the rich people enjoyed.

— "The ruin of Joseph" — the prophets went unheeded as they foretold a breakup of the Kingdom of Israel.

When we refuse to live in God's way, we bring trouble on ourselves.

Gospel Reading

In this parable we can see that Jesus is referring to the Jews' belief in life after death. We have a comparison between the rich and the poor in this world very much like the one given us by Amos.

— The Jews believed that there were two sections in Hades (or Sheol). In one section the dead waited quietly and peacefully for the resurrection and in the other the wicked were already being punished. How does Jesus use this idea in his parable?

— How can we see that the mere fact of being rich in this world does not guarantee a place in heaven? Do you think the story would have been different if the rich man had taken care of Lazarus instead of ignoring him?

— The Pharisees and others often asked Jesus to give them proof by signs that he was the Messiah and Jesus always refused. How does Jesus bring out this same refusal in the parable?

Prayer

Let us spend a few moments asking God to show us how to desire the real happiness he means for us. If we have all we need, let us be grateful and generous to others.

> "Father, help us to hurry toward the eternal life you promise and come to share in the joys of your kingdom."

27th Sunday of the Year   *Cycle C*

INCREASE OUR FAITH

Prepare your Bible

New Testament: 2 Timothy, ch. 1, vv. 6-8, 11-14.
St Luke, ch. 17, vv. 5-10.

First Reading

This is taken from the Book of Habakkuk. The persecuted people of his time were being encouraged to hold on to their faith in God's power to rescue them.

Second Reading

St Paul was writing to Timothy from his prison in Rome.

— What indicated that Paul had ordained Timothy?

— What particular gifts of the Spirit does Timothy seem to need?

— v. 14 is a lovely verse that we can apply to ourselves. Talk about it for a few moments. How can we guard this life of God within us?

Gospel Reading

— vv. 5, 6. A little faith can achieve great things. It is God who has almighty power — he asks us to believe in him.

— God made us and we belong to him. If he had not thought of us and created us in love, we would not be here. How grateful we should be! At the Offertory of the Mass when we bring bread and wine as signs of our thanks for life, they are not our own — they are gifts from God.

— vv. 7-10. Read these verses which help us to understand that we can never be thankful enough to God our Father.

Prayer

Share with each other some of the things you are grateful for. God's love and care come to us through events and people.

Use this Entrance Antiphon as a final prayer together:

> O Lord, you have given everything its place in the world, and no one can make it otherwise. For it is your creation, the heavens and the earth and the stars: you are the Lord of all.

28th Sunday of the Year   **Cycle C**

THANKSGIVING

Things you need

You might be able to find an appeal in the paper for a leprosy fund.

Prepare your Bible

Old Testament: 2 Kings, ch. 5, vv. 14-17.
New Testament: St Luke, ch. 17, vv. 11-19.

First Reading

You will remember that Naaman had travelled a long way to obtain his cure from the prophet Elisha. At first he was offended and insulted by the treatment that was suggested. It seemed too easy and humble for him.

— How was Naaman cured of his leprosy?

— How did he want to show his gratitude to Elisha?

— Why do you think Elisha refused to be rewarded?

— Naaman realised that although there was only one true God for all the world, yet the people of Israel had a special relationship with this God. Why did Naaman want to build his altar with soil from the land of Israel?

— Have you ever brought back a souvenir from a place you have visited? Why did you do so?

Gospel Reading

Lepers were very sad and lonely people in the time of Jesus because no cure was known for them and, because of infection, they had to live apart from everyone else.

— How can you tell from these verses that they respected the rule of isolation?

— The only people with authority were the priests. They had to make rulings on all kinds of problems. At what moment were the lepers cured? How did they show their faith in Jesus?

— Only one man said 'Thank you' at once. He was the Samaritan. What did strict Jews think about the people of Samaria? (cf. 13th and 15th Sunday of the Year, Cycle C).

— What did Jesus say to the man who realised he had been cured?

Prayer

Bad temper, selfishness, jealousy are catching. Jesus Christ never asks us to keep away from him when we are in one of these moods. Rather he says: "Come to me". Before we go to receive him in Holy Communion, we say:

"Lord, I am not worthy to receive you;
but only say the word and I shall be healed".

Let us ask for the grace to know our need of Jesus and to come to him with faith that he will heal us.

29th Sunday of the Year Cycle C

KEEP ON PRAYING

Things you need

(If you have young children). A pouffe or stool or box for Moses to sit on.

Prepare your Bible

Old Testament: Exodus, ch. 17, vv. 8-13.
New Testament: St Luke, ch. 18, vv. 1-8.

First Reading

The leader should decide who will read the parts of Moses and who will play the parts of Aaron and Hur.

— During their long journey to the Promised Land, the children of Israel ran into many difficulties. Not least were the constant attacks of marauding tribes similar to the one we read about today. Read and act the passage. Who was Moses' commander? Who were the attackers?

Response to the psalm

"Our help is in the name of the Lord who made heaven and earth".

Listen to the psalm at Mass and notice the confidence in God's power which the psalmist feels.

This response is used when a Bishop gives his blessing. It is full of trust in God's loving care.

Gospel Reading

Read the story which Jesus told about a judge who was not usually just and fair to his clients.

— What made this judge take the widow's case seriously?
— God seems to have a special interest in those who cannot look after themselves. Perhaps the widow could not afford to pay high fees. That kind of consideration does not enter into God's way of acting. We have only to pray and we are sure of God's action on our behalf.

Prayer

After we have all said the 'Our Father' at Mass, the priest continues:

> Deliver us, Lord, from every evil,
> and grant us peace in our day.
> In your mercy keep us free from sin
> and protect us from all anxiety
> as we wait in joyful hope
> for the coming of our Saviour, Jesus Christ.
> (What more could we ask of God!)
> For the kingdom, the power, and the glory are yours,
> now and for ever.
> (What faith in God this shows!)

30th Sunday of the Year   *Cycle C*

GOD HEARS OUR PRAYER

Prepare your Bible

Old Testament: Ecclesiasticus, ch. 35, vv. 12-14, 16-19.
New Testament: 2 Timothy, ch. 4, vv. 6-8, 16-18.
St Luke, ch. 18, vv. 9-14.

First Reading

— How can we tell that those in authority, when these words were written, did not care about justice for the seemingly unimportant?
— What kind of person serves God best?
— How should we make our prayers of petition to God?

Second Reading

— St Paul is writing to Timothy from prison. He knows that his life is nearing its end but he is triumphant. Why?

— When does Paul say that he specially felt God's power giving him strength?

— Paul does not fear death. He knows that death comes when God decides to call us to himself. How does this help him not to be afraid?

Gospel Reading

Jesus worked really hard trying to convince the Pharisees of their need for repentance. He longed for them to accept him and so find happiness.

— What particular fault in the Pharisees was Jesus trying to point out to them by telling this parable?

— Sometimes we can act like this Pharisee. Can you add to these possible comparisons.

> I always wear a clean shirt to school, not like . . .
> I never forget my dinner money, like . . .
> I always give up sweets during Lent, not like . . .
> I never bang the door like . . .

— God knows what goes on in our hearts. It is the love in our hearts for God and for other people that counts. The more we know our need for God and we ask him to help us, the more he will come close to us and fill us with himself.

A prayer from the psalm

> I will bless the Lord at all time.
> The Lord is close to the broken-hearted;
> those whose spirit is crushed he will save.
> Lord, help us to love you with all our hearts.
> Keep us from showing off and comparing ourselves
> to others.
> "What you think of me matters to me, O God, more than
> than anything else — how much you know about
> me!" (from Ps. 139. Alan Dale.)

TURN ROUND

Prepare your Bible

Old Testament: Wisdom, ch. 11, vv. 22 — ch. 12, v. 2.
New Testament: 2 Thessalonians, ch. 1, v. 1 — ch. 2, v. 2.
St Luke, ch. 19, vv. 1-10.

First Reading

— v. 22. How tiny is a grain of dust or a drop of dew! If the world seems like that to God, how great he must be!

— Read of the wonderful love God has for his creation. His love brought everything into being. This includes ME. Pause for a moment to think of this.

— Which verse speaks of God's spirit within us so that we will never die? What does this mean?

— ch. 2, vv. 1, 2. God's immense love for us makes it obvious that he wants us to be happy. How can we tell that his correction of our faults is for our good and made very gently?

Second Reading

— See how St Paul takes for granted a Christian's desire to make God known and loved.

As we approach the end of the Church's year, this reading invites us to begin to think about the Coming of Jesus Christ which we celebrate during Advent.

— The end of the world has still not come, nineteen hundred years after St Paul wrote this. The early Christians were constantly ready for Christ to come again. Perhaps we should take a leaf out of their book!

Gospel Reading

Tax collectors were disliked by the Jews because they worked for the Romans who were occupying Israel at this time. In spite of his high position, Zacchaeus was not too proud to take an unusual measure to try to see Jesus.

— What did he do?

— Do you think he hoped to go unnoticed?

— What do you think he felt when Jesus invited himself to supper?
— How did he decide to "turn round" in order to become a friend and follower of Jesus?
— Who are the "they" who objected to Jesus being entertained by Zacchaeus?
— Why is this a good story to read before we celebrate the Sacrament of Reconciliation?

Prayer

> Almighty and ever-living God,
> strengthen our faith, hope and love.
> May we do with loving hearts what you ask of us
> and come to share the life you promise.

32nd Sunday of the Year   *Cycle C*

HEAVEN IS OURS

Prepare your Bible

Old Testament: 2 Maccabees, ch. 7, vv. 1-2, 9-14.
New Testament: St Luke, ch. 20, vv. 27-38.

First Reading

The Book of the Maccabees is important because it affirms the belief in the resurrection. This passage also shows the Jews believed in the value of dying as a martyr in order to safeguard the faith in the one true God. The events described in these verses could be paralleled to the sufferings of the martyrs in the time of the Reformation and of some of the people who died in concentration camps within living memory.

— Why would these seven brothers not eat pork?
— How did the second brother show that he was looking forward to everlasting life?
— How did the third brother show that he knew that God was his creator and so that he owed all things to him?
— We read in other verses that the brave mother "endured resolutely because of her hopes in the Lord". You might like to read vv. 20-23.

Gospel Reading

The Sadducees were priests who did not believe in life after death. In this, they disagreed with the Pharisees. One thing that united them was their distrust and dislike of Jesus. This question, like many others, was put to Jesus in order to test him and put him in difficulties. Jesus had no problem in answering them.

— v. 37. By speaking of Abraham, Isaac and Jacob who all lived at different times, yet who could all claim to have the same God, Jesus shows that life must go on.

— v. 38. All men are alive to God. Here is the mystical body of Christ. Those in heaven, those on the way to heaven in purgatory and those still living on earth are all alive to God. That is why we can pray for each other. In the month of November we think especially of those who have died and we believe our prayers can help those in purgatory. We believe that our friends in heaven can pray for us.

Prayer

— Remember those who have died in the peace of Christ and all the dead whose faith is known to you alone.

(Eucharistic Prayer IV)

— Lord,
welcome into your kingdom our departed brothers and sisters, and all who have left this world in your friendship.
There we hope to share in your glory
when every tear shall be wiped away.
On that day we shall see you, our God, as you are.
We shall become like you
and praise you for ever through Christ our Lord,
from whom all good things come.

(Eucharistic Prayer III)

33rd Sunday of the Year   **Cycle C**

CHRIST IS VICTORIOUS

Things you need

Arrange your crucifix and a lighted candle with a picture of the Eucharist.

Prepare your Bible

Old Testament: Malachi, ch. 3, vv. 19-20.
New Testament: St Luke, ch. 21, vv. 5-19.

First Reading

This is taken from the last book of the Old Testament. It tells us of the time when Christ will rule in all men's hearts — when his kingdom will come on earth.

— v. 19. Fire was often taken as a sign of God's presence. Can you think of a time when the escaping children of Israel were aware of God in this way?

— Have you ever seen farmers burning their stubble? Why do they do this? How does this fit with the meaning of this verse?

— v. 20. To whom does the "sun of righteousness" refer? Sometimes "healing in his rays" is written as "healing in his wings". Which do you like best?

Gospel Reading

If St Luke wrote his Gospel after the year 70 AD, he would have been influenced in his memory of the words of Jesus by the actual capture and burning down of Jerusalem about this time.

Our greatest interest in this passage on Sunday is the way Jesus talks about the end of the world. Shall we concentrate on that aspect?

— What signs in nature will precede the end of the world?

— What kind of sufferings will Christians have to endure before the kingdom of Christ reigns over all the world?

— v. 16. Parents may be able to remember countries where this very thing happened in families.

— v. 14. We usually think of the Holy Spirit guiding our thoughts and words. But the Holy Spirit is the Spirit of Jesus so it makes no difference which phrase we use.

— vv. 18, 19 speak of our complete safety as friends and followers of Jesus Christ.

Prayer

Let us pray for those who suffer for their faith:

— for those who are not free to practise their faith,

— for ourselves, that we may be faithful in loving and serving God to the end of our lives.

215

CHRIST THE KING

— see page 82